FIFTY WOODEN BOATS

A CATALOG OF BUILDING PLANS

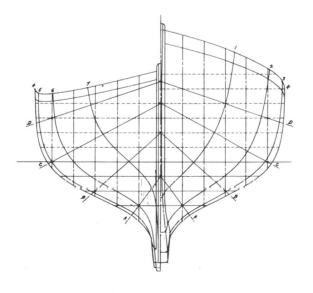

**By The Editors
of
WoodenBoat Magazine**

A Catalog of Building Plans

WoodenBoat

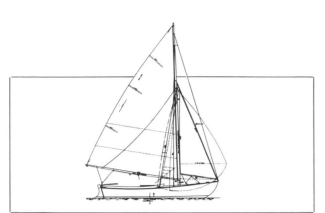

18'3" Sloop, O-Boat, by John G. Alden

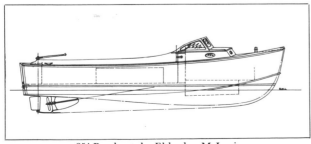

25' Bassboat, by Eldredge-McInnis

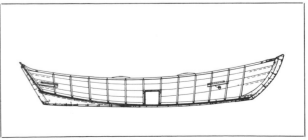

12'4" Yankee Tender, by WoodenBoat

Introduction

A catalog of study plans is at once food for thought, and fuel for endless hours of dreaming. At their best, such plans allow us to clearly compare varieties of hull shapes and rigs, and to feel ourselves fitting into carefully sketched-out accommodations. We can compare high-performance rowing shells with traditional dinghies for oar and sail. We can smell the cedar shavings, and know the pride of a well-placed plank. We can feel at once the anticipation and accomplishment.

At WoodenBoat, we have endeavored over the years to assemble a broad and diverse collection of plans for sale. We have attempted to select the designs for their utility, their beauty, their relative ease of construction, the clarity of their plans, and their accessibility. In some cases, we have commissioned designs to meet particular needs in distinctive ways, and in others, we have included designs as much for their educational value as for their suitability to specific requirements.

There are many fine designers whose works are not included in this first 50-boat collection, and many more fine designs than we can ever hope to include in future collections. But we have not attempted to suggest that this is the last word on anything. Indeed, it is only a beginning. We have selected these plans because we believe in them, and believe that they should be more widely available. We offer them for sale through WoodenBoat because we believe that the more good wooden boats in the world, the better for everyone. As agents for the designers whose works are included, we have a responsibility to encourage good workmanship in every respect, and to that end, the research and technical departments at WoodenBoat remain ready to assist builders with answers to questions and references to further readings in the literature.

More than just a catalog of building plans, *Fifty Wooden Boats* includes a discussion on understanding boat plans, an illustrated glossary of the structure of a wooden boat, a guide to alternative woods for boat construction, and a bibliography of books and articles on methods and materials in wooden boatbuilding. The format has been well accepted, and since we first published *Fifty Wooden Boats*, we have added two new plans books: *Thirty Wooden Boats* and *Forty Wooden Boats.* Our hope is that these volumes are both entertaining and informative, and that there are more than enough designs to consider. They were created for the builders and dreamers among us. Here's to both!

Jon Wilson, Editor
WoodenBoat Magazine

Understanding a Boat Plan

by Weston Farmer

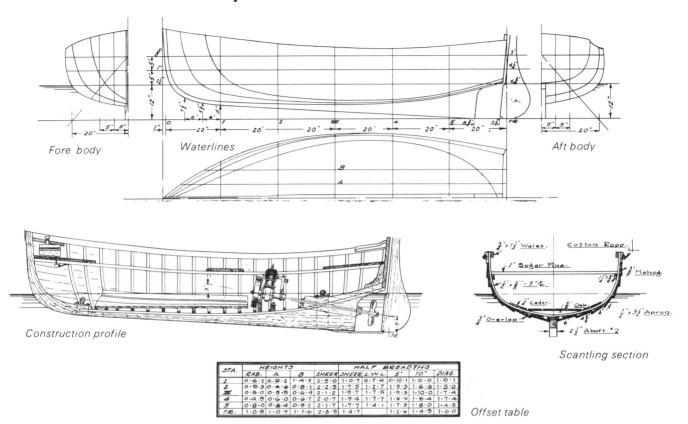

Fore body   Waterlines   Aft body

Construction profile

Scantling section

STA.	HEIGHTS				HALF BREADTHS				
	RAB.	A	B	SHEER	SHEER	L.W.L.	5"	10"	DIAG.
1	0·6·2	0·9·2	1·4·2	2·5·0	1·0·7	0·7·4	0·10·1	1·0·0	1·0·1
2	0·5·3	0·6·6	0·8·1	2·2·5	1·7·5	1·2·7	1·5·3	1·6·6	1·5·0
3	0·5·0	0·5·5	0·6·4	2·1·2	1·9·7	1·7·5	1·9·3	1·10·0	1·7·4
4	0·4·5	0·6·0	0·6·7	2·0·7	1·9·4	1·7·7	1·9·5	1·9·4	1·7·4
5	0·8·0	0·8·4	0·9·2	2·1·7	1·7·7	1·4·1	1·7·3	1·8·0	1·4·5
7R.	1·0·5	1·0·7	1·1·6	2·3·5	1·4·7		1·2·6	1·4·5	1·0·0

Offset table

A boat obviously is a three-dimensional structure. But the paper on which it is drawn is *two-dimensional*. The boat has form—length, breadth, depth. Paper is flat. It is the naval architect's job to depict on two-dimensional paper the shape that his boat must have to become, at the hands of the builder, the formed thing the architect designs.

To show the builder what he has in mind, the designer supplies a *lines drawing* which shows the boundary planes of the hull. He also supplies an *offset table*. The offsets are measurements for the lines from center *out* and from baseline *up* to points on the outboard face of the planking—measurements set off from center and base.

Custom has found it of most convenience to tabulate these measurements in three simple digits, reading in *feet*, *inches*, and *eighths*. Thus the figure 1-3-5 in an offset table reads one foot, three and five-eighths inches: $1'3^5/8''$. In addition to the lines drawing and the offset table, which enable a builder to lay down or loft the boat at full size, various other drawings are supplied.

Always, a *construction profile* must be shown. This is the inboard profile of structural elements shown as though the boat were split in two along the center of the keel and stem. A further key to the inboard profile is always given. This is the *scantling section*. It shows in cross dimension the sizes and outward locations of the elements shown on the inboard profile. This trio of drawings is all a knowing boatbuilder wants or needs to construct the average small boat.

An *outboard profile* drawing is given in nearly all but the simplest boats to show the external aspect afloat. In larger boats such as a cruiser or a runabout where there are several levels of construction when viewed from top down in plan, the *plan of framing* is shown. This plan shows framing, floors, deck framing, cabin sole (flooring) framing, and disposition of parts in the joinerwork scheme.

In such larger boats, usually more cross sections are shown to give the builder information as to where these pieces of joinerwork go and how they are put together; hence, these views are termed *joiner sections*.

As far as the builder goes, probably the most important plan is the lines drawing, for (in most cases) the *boat must be laid out full-size* on the shop floor or on a piece of building paper before the rigid mold or backbone on which the boat is framed can be built.

To learn by example how to "read" a set of boat drawings and why they are drawn as you see them, take a good long look at the set of lines heading the opening page of this article. This set of lines is for a little 10′ power dinghy. She is an inboard power boat. Her construction profile, scantling section, and table of offsets are shown on this page. From the information given, you have all that the average boatyard asks for in building information—you could build a nice little-boy's launch from these plans.

Because she is a boat of normal form, very small and hence understandable, and, being round-bottomed, which seems to bother most beginners, her drawings will serve ideally as a guide in explaining the starting point to you. (Her name is IRREDUCIBLE.)

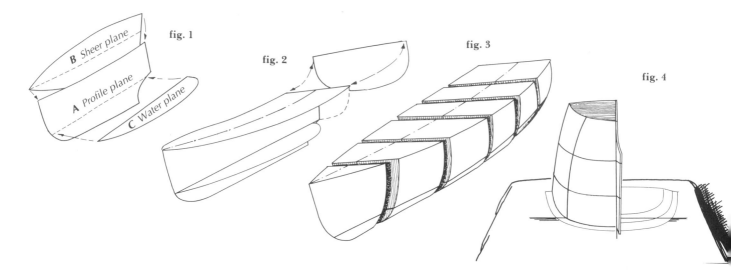

Now look at Figure 1. This shows the profile plan "A," with which the designer starts. The profile plan is the boundary line showing stem profile, transom rake, keel outline, and the character of the sheerline.

To give this silhouette three-dimensional form, imagine the sheer or deck plan cut out of cardboard, the outline of which gives boundary to the width of the boat as at "B," Figure 1. To give further outer hull limits, also imagine the shape for the waterline, and we have the water plane boundary as at "C," Figure 1.

So on the equivalent flat paper drawing of IRREDUCIBLE, we would now have—in dimensions—the profile only. And below it in plan, we have the outline and the load waterline.

Now our boat begins to take on form. To fill it in, imagine as in Figure 2, that the boundary planes of sheer plan, profile, and waterline all jump into proper three-dimensional relationship, If we can also imagine a pleasing transom shape and glue it astern by imagination, our vessel takes more definite form.

The naval architect gives his boat its final bulk by shaping up the sections. If we now cut the bulk into sections as in Figure 3, we get an idea of the change of hull shape from point to point along the profile.

If this stack of sections were now placed at a common center and a common waterline on flat paper as in Figure 4, and the outline of each section were drawn on the paper, we would have a two-dimensional record of the sections necessary to recreate the boat we wanted.

This would give us the fore body sections and the after body sections. It is usual to show only the sections for *half* a boat, as both sides are always symmetrical.

If we turned the boat in plan and pressed it through the paper, leaving a record of the horizontal boundaries, we'd have a deck line and a waterline. But *one* waterline isn't enough to give a builder the information he needs for laying out sections. He needs more checkpoints.

So the designer gives us more waterlines. In IRREDUCIBLE, two waterlines are drawn in at 5" and 10" above the load waterline. You get the plan shape of these from the sectional views drawn beneath the profile. A baseline, 12" below the load waterline, is also drawn in to give a point of departure for heights of the intersections. But this still isn't enough.

You need checkpoints between waterline and the keel rabbet. So the designer uses what are termed *buttock lines*. These are slices through the hull in vertical plane, outboard of center.

In this design the buttock lines are 5" apart. This gives you points on the sectional plan by which you can locate the sweep of the mold sections from keel rabbet to waterline.

To tie all of these checkpoints together, and to prove fairness, a designer frequently slices the hull, as though with a bandsaw on a solid model, by a diagonal line. Sometimes these diagonal lines are projected in plan view. To skilled eyes, they tell much of performance, particularly with sailing vessels.

In IRREDUCIBLE the diagonals are not projected down, serving merely in the offset table as additional locating points for the sectional shapes.

To sum up: Each of the lines in the lines drawing represents the boundary of a *plane* passing through the hull shape. By measuring off these points with reference to a centerline and a baseline, you can reproduce at full size on the floor of your shop the boat the designer intended. Why must you do this?

You do it to mechanically save a lot of time, to avoid errors. There is *no other way* to build a boat if it is built from plans. The reason is simple: the boat has planking and frames; she has a transom. All these are shown in the construction profile and scantling section. All these pieces must go together and fit.

The stem is rabbeted for the hood ends of the planking (see Figure 6). The transom must be expanded to true (instead of projected) size and beveled for the stream the planks will take (see Figure 8). The planking has thickness and so do the frames. These must be *subtracted* from the outside hull shape the architect draws (see Figure 10).

All of this is (generally) done *full size*. You can't scale a small blueprint $1/12$th or $1/16$th the size of the boat and get the necessary bevels, nor fair cross sections.

Further, a stem must be got out. Usually you do this by transferring the lofted line to the lumber by inserting nailheads around the line and hammering the character of the curve into the lumber. This is shown in Figure 7.

Templates for cutting knees and the keel and shaft log are needed. And if they are to go together, you must take them from an integral master loft drawing. If there were no other reasons but these for laying down the boat full size, it would be enough for a good mechanic.

Once laid down full size, the shape of the hull has integrity and matches the lines drawing, and the main pieces of hull frame such as stem, knees, and expanded transom, are in size to transfer to lumber.

At this point, for the novice, the only seeming constructional mysteries have to do with getting out the stem and

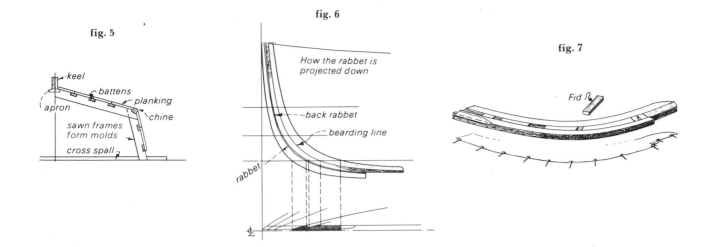

fig. 5

fig. 6

fig. 7

expanding the transom. Figure 6 shows how you project the waterlines on the profile down to the half siding of the keel to stream into the stem. By drawing in the planking thickness behind the plan waterlines, you can find the lay of the rabbet, the back rabbet, and the bearding line.

As shown in Figure 8, if the transom is on a raked angle, it must be expanded. This merely means it must be drawn to real size.

If you were to project the transom as shown in the aft body plan in strict elevation as shown to the left in Figure 8, then build the transom to this outline, you'd find it too small, because you would not have allowed for the slant, or rake. The drawing is self-explanatory.

Boats have dozens of types of construction. Hulls may be round or V-shaped. But the basic idea behind the plan, when you start to build, is to get the correct shape for the hull. Then, as shown in Figure 9, provide a secure set of forms on which to frame and plank the boat.

For some reason, the V-bottomed seam-and-batten type of boat, shown in Figure 5, is readily understood by beginners. The frames of the boat itself, and the battens, are left in and become an integral part. Such construction takes nice lofting, and the frames must be beveled and faired to a hair.

The professional boatbuilder, using methods evolved by his craft over thousands of years, makes an easier thing of building by preferring to build round-bottomed boats. The form, as at Figure 9, can be built of junk lumber, the ribbands over which the frames are bent by that most useful device, steaming, can all be thrown together so they fair themselves, and the resulting boat, being made of smaller and more pliable pieces, is easier to build.

Small boats like the one shown usually are built *bottom up* as they can be easily turned over, and building thus is easier on the back; provides down drive for fastenings; is immediately ready for planing and sanding.

The boat shown progressing in Figure 9 shows the clinker planking method forward. In this method, the strakes are clinker fastened about the molds, and then the frames are steam-bent in later.

The aft half of the boat framed in Figure 9 is being planked carvel, or smooth seamed. For this, the setup of the molds is shown in Figure 10. This is depicted merely to bring home the point about lofting: Notice that the thickness of the planking has been subtracted, then the thickness of the frames, then the thickness of the ribbands over which the frames are bent. The resulting mold is much smaller than the designer's body plan.

fig. 8

How the transom is drawn full or actual size

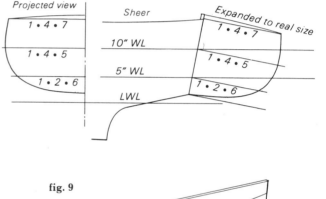

fig. 9

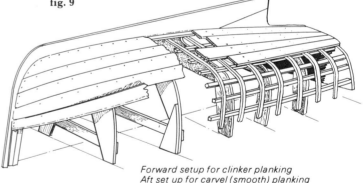

Forward setup for clinker planking
Aft set up for carvel (smooth) planking

fig. 10

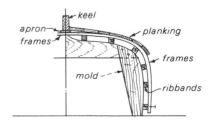

This article was excerpted from *WoodenBoat* No. 21.

7'7" Sailing Pram, Nutshell

by Joel White

PARTICULARS

LOA	7'7"
Beam	4'
Draft (cb up)	5"
(cb down)	1'9"
Weight	about 90 lbs
Sail area:	37 sq ft

The Nutshell Pram is, in our opinion, one of the best tenders ever designed. She's a beauty in looks, easy to build, and does her job far, far better than most boats of her length. She rows very easily, and can carry three adults with a comfortable margin of freeboard. She tracks exceptionally well, and even in a chop against a breeze she holds her own like a true pulling boat. The Nutshell tows steadily and with little disturbance. An ideal yacht tender, she can also be rigged to sail. Very stable yet swift under her lug sail, she's a great "fun" boat for kids and adults alike.

Joel White, who created the design, has this to say about the Nutshell Pram: "Little boats are fun to develop, but not easy, since the design constraints are so strong, and the requirements so firm.... One of the requirements was that it must be constructed from 8' plywood panels, so the pram became 7'7" overall. An earlier plywood pulling boat I built with glued laps proved to be such a success that the same construction is used here in Nutshell. It produces a strong, light, easily constructed hull, and one that is so uncluttered inside that cleaning and painting become easy."

The Nutshell Pram is planked upside down on a building jig. Consisting of only 22 wooden parts (Rowing model), the design was a natural for a kit, and WoodenBoat first offered her as a complete kit boat, one of the most attractive and best performing for her size of any we've seen. (The Nutshell Pram Kit is still available in a Rowing Model for $700.00, and a Sailing Model for $895.00, freight collect.)

In WB No. 60, we ran a "how-to-build" article on the Nutshell, and we now offer a plans package for those who prefer to furnish their own material. The plans consist of eight sheets, including building jig details, template sheet, scaled plank patterns, patterns for structural members, and construction details. A how-to build manual and video can be purchased separately. WB Plan No. 41. $75.00.

Plan 41

DESCRIPTION
Hull type: Flat-bottomed, pram type
Rig: Lug
Construction: Glued lapstrake plywood
PERFORMANCE
*Suitable for: Protected waters
*Intended capacity: 1-3
Trailerable: Yes
Propulsion: Oars or sail

*See page 112 for further information.

Speed (knots):   3
BUILDING DATA:
Skill needed: Basic
Lofting required: No
*Alternative construction: None
"How to Build" instructions: monograph or video
PLANS DATA
No. of sheets: 8
Level of detail: Extreme
Cost per set: $75.00
WB Plan No. 41

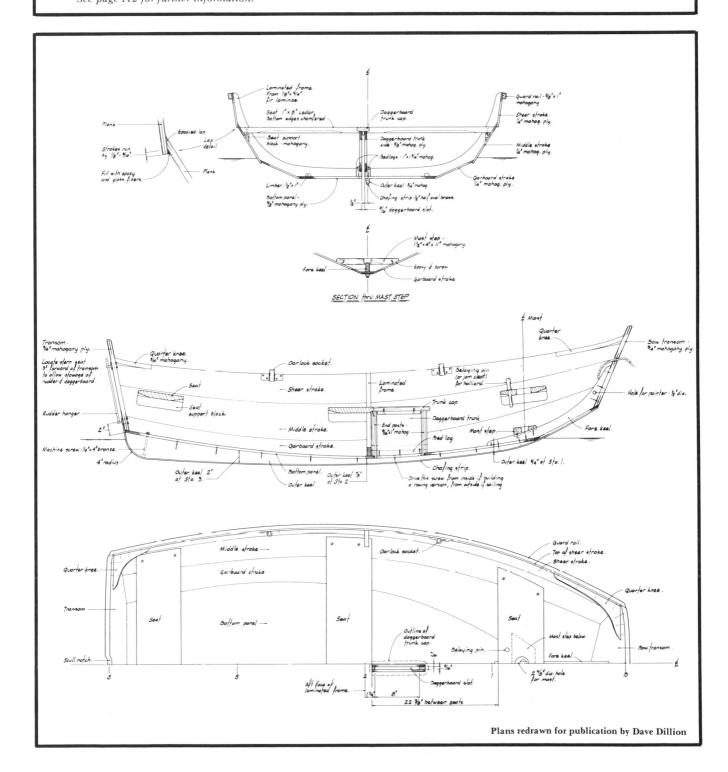

Plans redrawn for publication by Dave Dillion

9'6" Sailing Pram, Nutshell

by Joel White

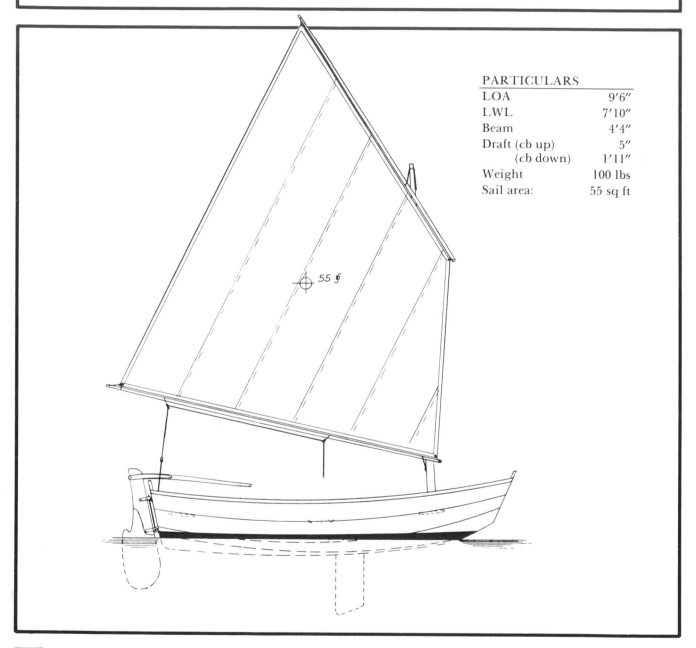

PARTICULARS	
LOA	9'6"
LWL	7'10"
Beam	4'4"
Draft (cb up)	5"
(cb down)	1'11"
Weight	100 lbs
Sail area:	55 sq ft

The success of the 7'7" Nutshell Pram convinced us all that the same general shape and method of construction would work just as well in a larger boat; thus a bigger, 9½' Nutshell was created. With 2' more length and 4" more beam, she can carry a bigger load, hold more people, handle a proportionally larger sail, and has far more stability. Under oars or sail, she slides along every bit as well, and the added length increases her maximum speed with either means of propulsion.

This new and bigger Nutshell has the same easy-to-build lapstrake plywood hull that is virtually frameless (there's only a single laminated 'midship frame). She's rugged, she won't dry out when stored out of the water for long periods, and her smooth interior makes her easy to clean and paint.

Which size pram to select depends upon the use you'll be giving it, and upon your own priorities. For sailing comfort and performance, this 9½-footer is noticeably superior. She's very much more stable as well (you can stand on her rail without it going underwater). This boat will cost more to build, it tows a little harder, and it's heavier. And, of course, if you intend to carry it on deck or cabintop, the overall dimensions may make the decision for you.

The 9'6" Nutshell is also available in kit form: $950 for the Rowing Model and $1,195 for a Sailing Model. Both prams are easy to care for, once built.

The plans come in five sheets, including lines and off-sets, building jig, sailing rig details, construction, full-size lofting and templates. WB Plan No. 57. $75.00.

Plan 57

DESCRIPTION
Hull type: Multi-chined pram
Rig: Single lugsail
Construction: Glued lapstrake plywood

PERFORMANCE
*Suitable for: Protected waters
*Intended capacity: 3-4 rowing, 1-2 sailing
Trailerable: Yes

See page 112 for further information.

Propulsion: Oars, sail, outboard
Speed (knots):   3

BUILDING DATA:
Skill needed: Basic
Lofting required: No
*Alternative construction: None
"How to Build" instructions: monograph or video

PLANS DATA
No. of sheets: 5
Level of detail: Above average
Cost per set: $75.00
WB Plan No. 57

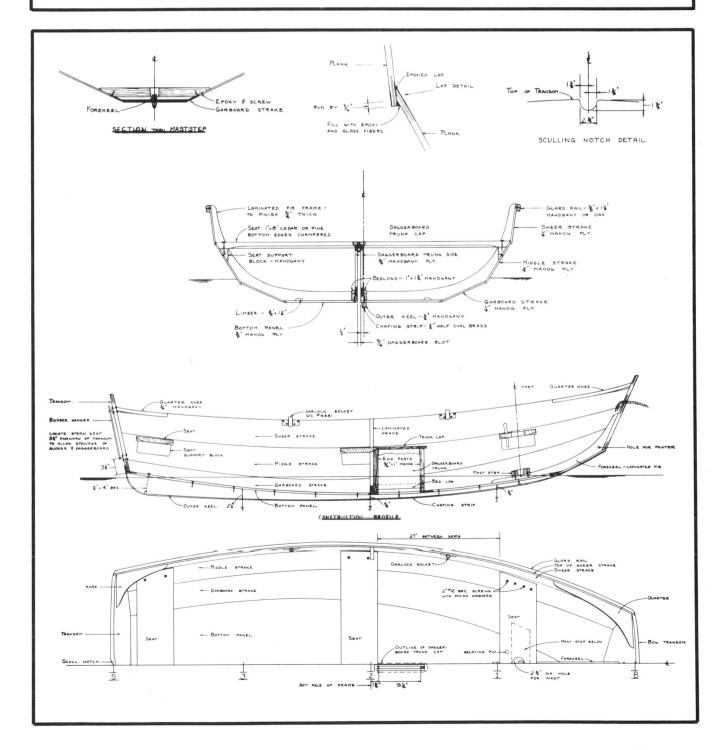

9'6" Skiff, Martha's Tender

by Joel White

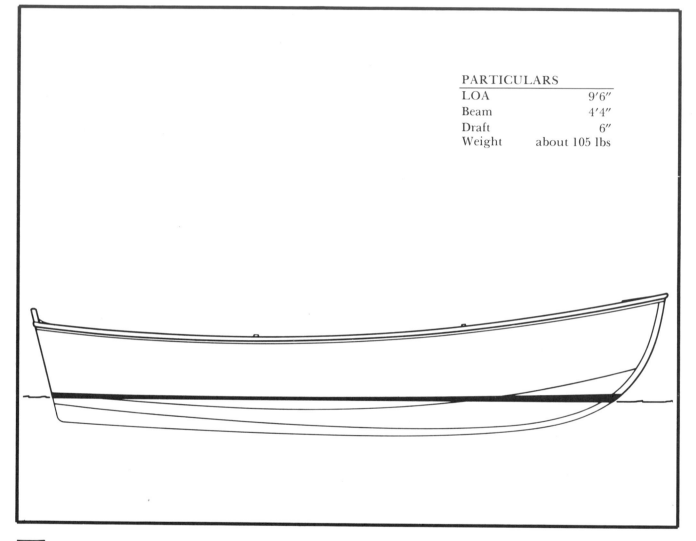

PARTICULARS

LOA	9'6"
Beam	4'4"
Draft	6"
Weight	about 105 lbs

This design is particularly well proven because so many boats have been built from it over the years. Both fishermen and yachtsmen have found what they were after in these boats: robust carrying capacity, reasonably light weight, and reasonable initial cost. With its firm bilges and a full-length outer keel, people have found through experience that this is not a boat to scoot out from under them while stepping aboard. They've also found that she tows well and doesn't become a liability in a following sea.

WoodenBoat has been partial to this design for some time, and upon establishing its summer boatbuilding school in 1980, arranged to teach the building of Martha's Tender as one of its courses. From this experience, we have learned how quickly a beginner can build such a boat; the class averaged about one ready-to-be-painted boat for every two students each week—with capable instruction, of course. Working alone, you'd no doubt take longer—except that you're not really alone: A photo essay on building Martha's Tender, featured in WB Nos. 45, 46, and 47, provides very complete and well-illustrated building instruc-

tions. By following them, you'll be guided through each step of the process, and you'll find it's the next best thing to attending our school.

This V-bottomed plywood tender can be constructed from readily available materials. Her design was developed to make use of 10'-long panels of plywood, but if more length is desired, longer panels can be made up, and the building molds can be spaced out for a hull as long as 14'. The hull is built upside down over a temporary jig, making the usual sawn frames unnecessary and keeping the interior of the finished boat free from much of the structural clutter. Inside, she's fitted with three thwarts and two rowing stations. Outside, the hull is sheathed with fiberglass over its fir plywood planking for extra abrasion resistance and for a good surface for painting. Her transom can be notched for sculling, and she could even be fitted with a sailing rig and centerboard (although as yet there are no plans). Or, a small outboard could be used.

Plans come in three sheets: lines and offsets, construction, and jig detail. WB Plan No. 25. $45.00.

Plan 25

DESCRIPTION
Hull type: V-bottomed
Rig: None yet
Construction: Plywood

PERFORMANCE
*Suitable for: Protected waters
*Intended capacity: 3
Trailerable: Yes
Propulsion: Oars, outboard

* See page 112 for further information.

Speed (knots):   1-3

BUILDING DATA
Skill needed: Basic
Lofting required: No
*Alternative construction: None
Featured as "How to Build" article in WB Nos.
   45, 46, 47

PLANS DATA
No. of sheets: 3
Level of detail: Average
Cost per set: $45.00
WB Plan No. 25

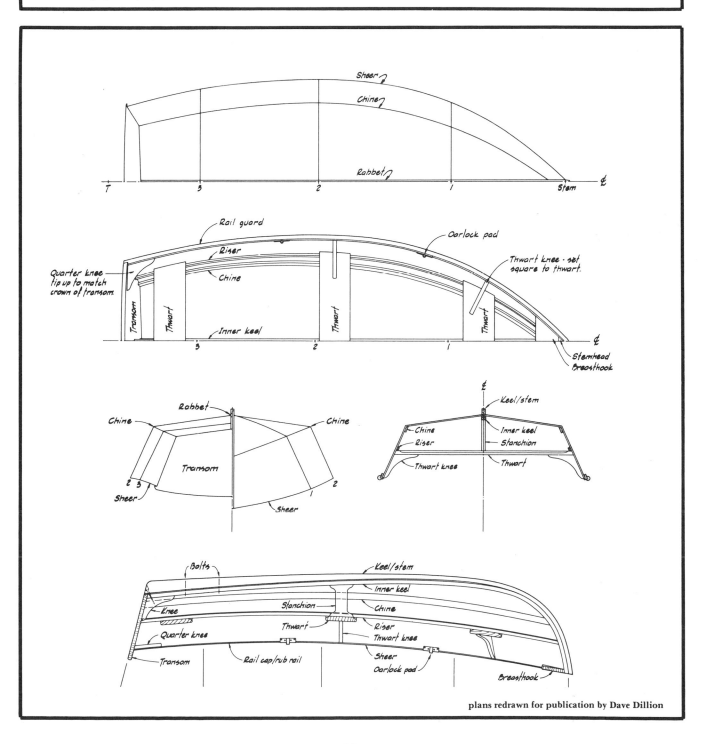

plans redrawn for publication by Dave Dillion

11'3" Skiff

by Asa Thomson

Plans drawn for publication by Spencer Lincoln

PARTICULARS

LOA	11'3"
Beam	4'5"
Weight	125-150 lbs

These plans are taken from what is thought to be the last remaining Asa Thomson flat-bottomed skiff, now owned by Mystic Seaport Museum. The Asa Thomson Skiff rows surprisingly well, and her rockered bottom makes her responsive as well as allowing her to carry three adults and still row well.

Mr. Thomson apparently built Mystic's skiff for a fisherman; there's a watertight bait well under the middle thwart, open to the sea through holes bored in the boat's bottom. Access is through two hinged lids that form the central part of the thwart when closed. It's a unique feature, adding enough strength through its bulkheads so the usual seat knees aren't required. Even if you're not a fisherman, you might still find the space useful as a dry compartment for secure and weatherproof storage of life jackets, oarlocks and other boat gear.

With an 11'3" LOA and a beam of 4'5", she weighs only about 150 pounds. The skiff at Mystic is framed in oak, double-planked with 3/8" white pine on her bottom and 3/8" white pine in three stakes on each side. She's fastened with copper clout nails. Her transom is 5/8" oak, and oak is also used for her stem, chines, sternpost, and seats. The keel piece, skeg, inwales, and guardrail are made of yellow birch, and natural apple crooks form the breasthook and quarter knees.

Although the plans for the Asa Thomson Skiff don't go into as much detail as the ones we've developed for the Yankee Skiff or the Catspaw Dinghy, there is ample information from which to build her.

Additional information on the skiff is available in an article entitled "Asa Thomson's Elegant Skiffs," WB No. 29. WB Plan No. 9. $20.00.

Plan 9

DESCRIPTION

Hull type: Flat-bottomed, straight flaring sides

Rig: None

Construction: Cross-planked bottom, lapstrake sides

Featured in WB No. 29

PERFORMANCE

*Suitable for: Protected waters

*Intended capacity: 3

* See page 112 for further information.

Trailerable: Yes

Propulsion: Oars

Speed (knots): 1-3

BUILDING DATA:

Skill needed: Intermediate

Lofting required: No

*Alternative construction: Plywood

PLANS DATA

No. of sheets: 1

Level of detail: Below average

Cost per set: $20.00

WB Plan No. 9

12'4" Yankee Tender

by WoodenBoat

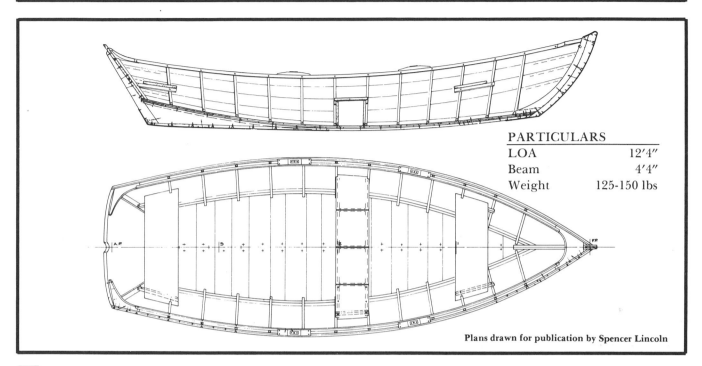

PARTICULARS	
LOA	12'4"
Beam	4'4"
Weight	125-150 lbs

Plans drawn for publication by Spencer Lincoln

Feeling that some improvements could be made on the original Asa Thomson Flat-Bottomed Skiff, Wooden-Boat (Maynard Bray, Spencer Lincoln, Joel White, and Jon Wilson) drew up some modified plans.

Mr. Thomson, a New Bedford boatbuilder legendary for his exacting standards and fine workmanship, built a number of skiff-tenders. Designed for a specific purpose in a specific area, they were light with a flat bottom for easy beaching. A good freeboard provided protection against a Buzzards Bay chop, and the strong sheer keeps the ends buoyant.

Feeling that Mr. Thomson's design was just a bit stubby (probably because he was obliged to keep the overall length down to a minimum for easy stowage), WoodenBoat raked both the stem and stern, keeping the same bottom length, and raised her out of the water a bit forward so that she'd tow better and run farther up the beach.

The original skiff by Mr. Thomson had three planks up each side. While it was easy for Asa Thomson to find wide planking in the 1920s, it's a different story today; Wooden-Boat felt obliged to use four planks on each side, and chose Maine cedar over the original white pine.

Like Mr. Thomson's, the Yankee Tender is light and responsive. She will carry three adults with ease and promises to be a good tender and fun for "poking about." LOA is 12'4", and her beam is 4'4". Her weight of less than 150 pounds makes her easy for two adults to carry, and she can be loaded on a trailer or truck.

WoodenBoat Nos. 30 and 31 feature "Building a Flat-Bottomed Skiff" from the Yankee Tender plans, using step-by-step details. The plans themselves are exceptionally detailed. WB Plan No. 11. $50.00.

Plan 11

DESCRIPTION
Hull type: Flat-bottomed, straight flaring sides
Rig: None
Construction: Cross-planked bottom, lapstrake sides

PERFORMANCE
*Suitable for: Protected waters
*Intended capacity: 3
Trailerable: Yes

See page 112 for further information.

Propulsion: Oars
Speed (knots): 1-3

BUILDING DATA
Skill needed: Basic
Lofting required: No
*Alternative construction: Plywood
Helpful WB issues: WB Nos. 30 & 31

PLANS DATA
No. of sheets: 5
Level of detail: Extreme
Cost per set: $50.00
WB Plan No. 11

11' Dinghy

by Charles Witholz

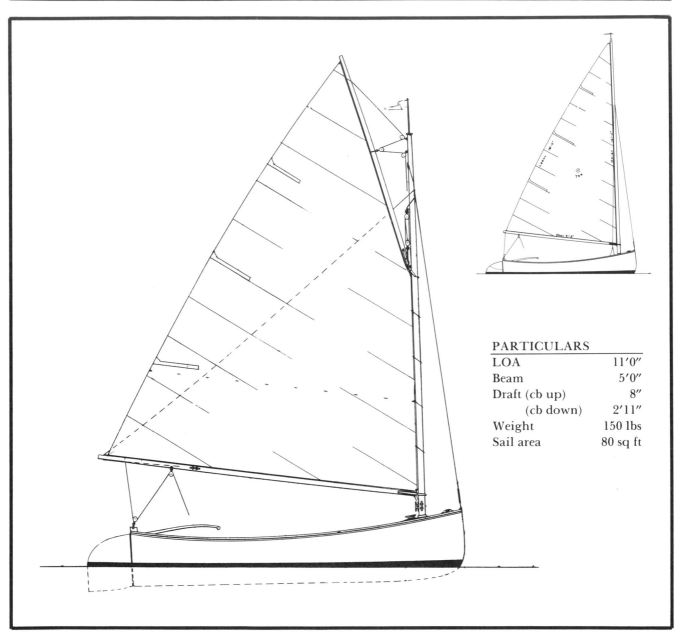

PARTICULARS

LOA	11'0"
Beam	5'0"
Draft (cb up)	8"
(cb down)	2'11"
Weight	150 lbs
Sail area	80 sq ft

Here is a beautifully modeled craft designed by a man with long experience in Cape Cod-type catboats. Witholz worked some catboat features into this design, as well as some features from the classic Whitehall. This dinghy is beamy at the rail for dryness, stability, and load carrying, yet narrow at the waterline so she'll slip easily through the water. Her bow and stern are shaped both for good performance and for good looks.

She was conceived for easy rowing and comfortable sailing—the kind of boat in which you tour a harbor, launching her from the davits of your powerboat or the deck of your sailing craft after an all-day run at sea. Or you can dry sail her from your garage where, because of her cold-molded construction, she'll live happily for as long as you wish without drying out and leaking when she's launched. She'd probably tow well in calm weather, but she was not meant to be an always-in-the-water yacht tender tethered to a towline when the going gets rough.

The plans let you choose between a daggerboard (which takes up less space inside the boat) or a pivoted centerboard (which is permanently rigged and ready for use; it doesn't hang up during grounding in shallow water). You also have a choice of rigs—either the traditional gaff or more modern marconi. The plans are well detailed and drawn with the amateur builder in mind. Lines and offsets are included for those who prefer to do their own lofting, or an optional full-size body plan may be purchased from the designer. WB Plan No. 50. $50.00.

Plan 50

DESCRIPTION
Hull type: Round-bottomed, with transom stern
and centerboard
Rig: Gaff or marconi cat
Construction: Cold-molded

PERFORMANCE
*Suitable for: Protected waters
*Intended capacity: 4

See page 112 for further information.

Trailerable: Yes
Propulsion: Sail, oars, small outboard
Speed (knots):   2-4

BUILDING DATA:
Skill needed: Intermediate
Lofting required: Optional
*Alternative construction: None

PLANS DATA
No. of sheets: 5
Level of detail: Above average
Cost per set: $50.00
WB Plan No. 50

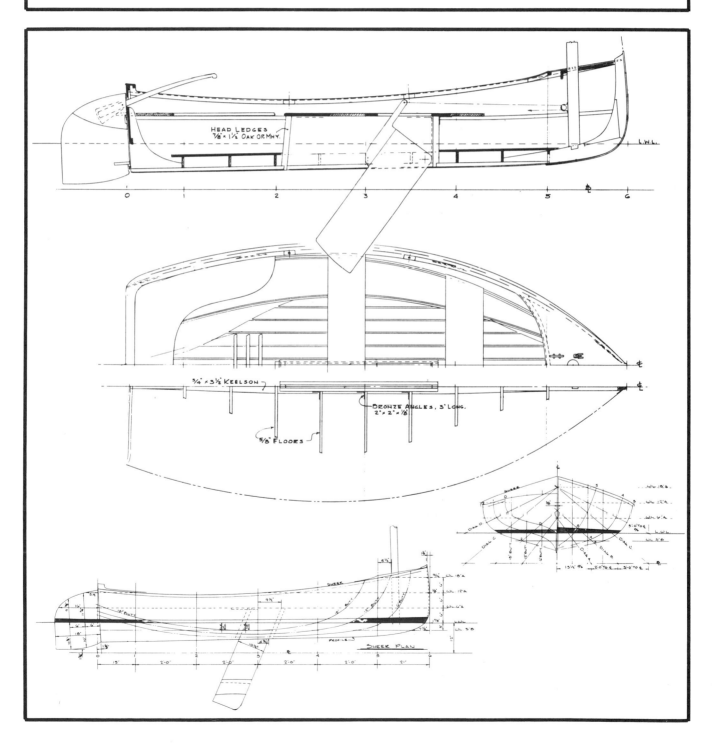

11'9" Acorn Skiff

by Iain Oughtred

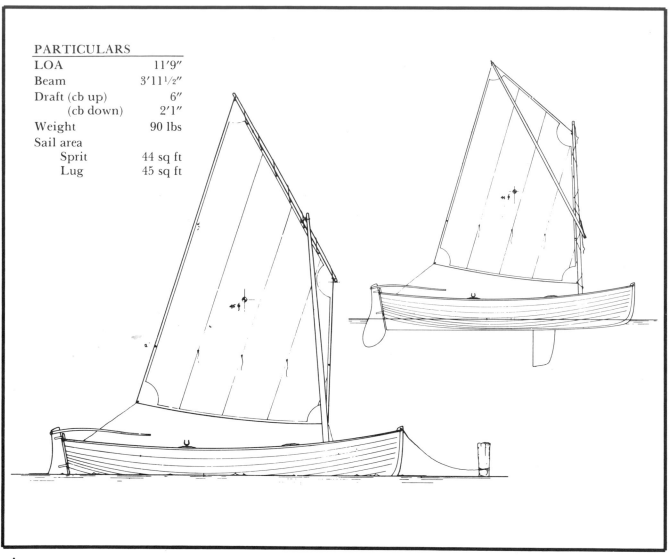

PARTICULARS	
LOA	11'9"
Beam	3'11½"
Draft (cb up)	6"
(cb down)	2'1"
Weight	90 lbs
Sail area	
Sprit	44 sq ft
Lug	45 sq ft

ACORN is an elegant Whitehall-type pulling boat built of lapstrake plywood. Although she's called a "skiff," her hull is round-bilged, not flat-bottomed, as is the case with most so-called "skiffs." For such a sophisticated shape, you'll find her easy to build, and the combination of simple construction, classic lines, light weight, and versatility make her a very successful blend of past and present. (See article & photos, WB No. 56.)

With narrow waterline and low freeboard (to keep down windage), ACORN was designed to handle easily and row smoothly, rather than to carry heavy loads. Her rising forefoot and lean hindquarters (ending in a pretty wineglass transom) allow her to tow well if used as a tender. She'll also sail when fitted with the sprit or lug rig, rudder, and daggerboard shown in the plans. Although she has an initial tenderness under sail (having been designed primarily as a rowboat), the ACORN Skiff will sail to windward and tack easily.

With the amateur boatbuilder in mind, British yacht designer Iain Oughtred designed ACORN for glued-lapstrake construction with marine plywood—a type of construction using readily available materials and one that does not require any riveting or steam-bending. (The curved pieces are composed of glued-up laminations, although they *could* be steam-bent.) The plywood planking is strong enough so that the usual clutter of internal framing has been virtually eliminated, making this skiff structurally clean and easier to refinish than the traditional lapstrake craft. Another advantage of dimensionally stable plywood with glued, lapped edges is that the skiff can be kept ashore for long periods of time without drying out and subsequently leaking. She'll even survive being stored upside down on top of the car.

The plans are beautifully detailed, and come in six sheets—lines and offsets, building jig, construction, details, sail plans, oars, and full-size patterns for the stem, transom, molds, knees, and floors. Illustrated step-by-step instructions are included as well. WB Plan No. 43. $80.00.

Plan 43

DESCRIPTION
Hull type: Round-bottomed, Whitehall-type with daggerboard
Rig: Sprit or standing lug
Construction: Glued lapstrake plywood

PERFORMANCE
*Suitable for: Protected waters
*Intended capacity: 1-3
Trailerable: Yes

See page 112 for further information.

Propulsion: Sail, oars
Speed (knots):   1-4

BUILDING DATA
Skill needed: Basic to intermediate
Lofting required: No
*Alternative construction: Carvel, strip, or cold-molded

PLANS DATA
No. of sheets: 6 plus instruction booklet
Level of detail: Above average
Cost per set: $80.00
WB Plan No. 43

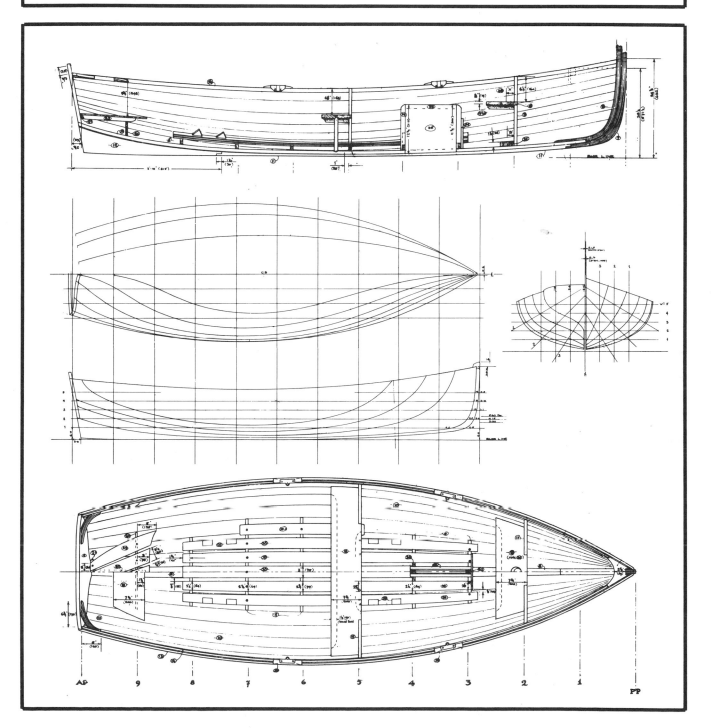

12' Dinghy

by Frederick Goeller

PARTICULARS

LOA	12'0"
Beam	4'3"
Draft (cb up)	9"
(cb down)	2'8"
Weight	175-225 lbs
Sail area:	83 sq ft

L. Francis Herreshoff felt that Frederick Goeller was one of the best draftsmen that he knew, and Mr. Goeller proved his design ability when he came up with this boat that will row, sail, and handle an outboard motor, plus be strong, beautiful, and practical at the same time! The plans for the 12' dinghy originally appeared in the book, *Rudder Sail Boat Plans,* published in 1948.

One could not imagine a better yacht tender of this size. Ruggedly constructed of cedar and oak (Douglas-fir, red-cedar, or yellow cedar could be alternative choices, but avoid hard mahogany), she has an excellent carrying capacity and good stability. She can carry three to four persons in relative comfort, more in calm conditions. Her handsome sailing rig will stow inside the boat, and her buoyancy aft makes it possible to tend a reasonable outboard without fear.

The Goeller Dinghy is a responsive boat in a good breeze and should be easy for children to sail. She's truly versatile.

Plans for the Goeller dinghy show good detail, and her construction will require a moderate amount of skill. She's featured in the "Designs" section of WB No. 25. The plans come in three sheets (lines and offsets, construction plan, sail plan and details). WB Plan No. 10. $40.00.

Plan 10

DESCRIPTION

Hull type: Round-bottomed, transom stern, centerboard

Rig: Single sliding gunter

Construction: Carvel planked over steamed frames

Featured in Design Section: WB No. 25

PERFORMANCE

*Suitable for: Protected waters

*Intended capacity: 2-4 daysailing

Propulsion: Oars, sail, outboard

Speed (knots):   2-4

BUILDING DATA:

Skill needed: Intermediate

Lofting required: Yes

*Alternative construction: Lapstrake, strip, or cold-molded

PLANS DATA

No. of sheets: 3

Level of detail: Average

Cost per set: $40.00

WB Plan No. 10

See page 112 for further information.

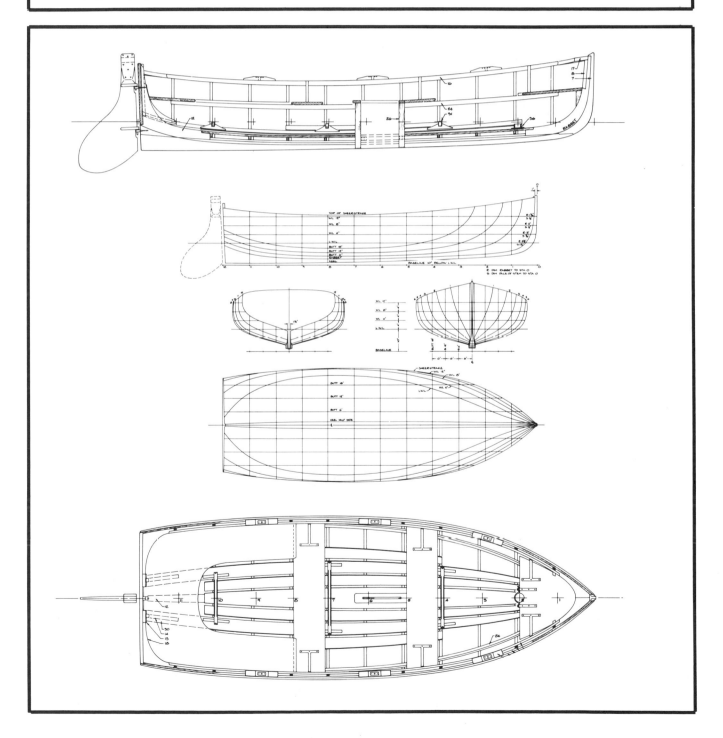

12'6" Marisol Skiff

by Gifford Jackson

PARTICULARS	
LOA	12'6"
Beam	4'7½"
Draft (cb up)	9"
(cb down)	2'4"
Weight	175-200 lbs
Sail area	70 sq ft

Marisol, meaning "sea and sun" in Spanish, was designed by Gifford Jackson of Auckland, New Zealand. He wanted a little day boat that he could launch and sail singlehandedly, but one that would also be artistically expressive. The boat that emerged looks rather like something out of the 18th century with her decorative color scheme, jaunty sheer, and details. Her construction is modern—glued plywood with laminated trim.

She is a V-bottomed boat with a 12'6" LOA. She can be sailed as a simple gunter-rigged catboat, rowed, or outboard powered. Marisol is lively and responsive in light and moderate airs; she's well suited to different conditions in the hands of careful sailors.

Mr. Jackson has defined the design in 25 pages of text and 35 sheets of detailed drawings. Marisol can be built by an amateur with some woodworking experience, but she provides a challenge for professionals as well. She is designed strictly for marine plywood construction and could be built either of Bruynzeel mahogany-faced marine plywood or fir marine plywood. Interior- or exterior-grade plywood should be avoided.

A more complete description of the boat is available in WB No. 12, "Something of My Own," by Gifford Jackson. WB Plan No. 13. $125.00.

Plan 13

DESCRIPTION
Hull type: V-bottomed, hard chine, centerboarder
Rig: Sliding gunter
Construction: Lapstrake plywood over sawn frames
Featured in WB No. 12

PERFORMANCE
*Suitable for: Protected waters
*Intended capacity: 2

*See page 112 for further information.

Trailerable: Yes
Propulsion: Oars, sail, or outboard
Speed (knots): 1-4

BUILDING DATA:
Skill needed: Basic to intermediate
Lofting required: No
*Alternative construction: None

PLANS DATA
No. of sheets: 35
Level of detail: Extreme
Cost per set: $125.00
WB Plan No. 13

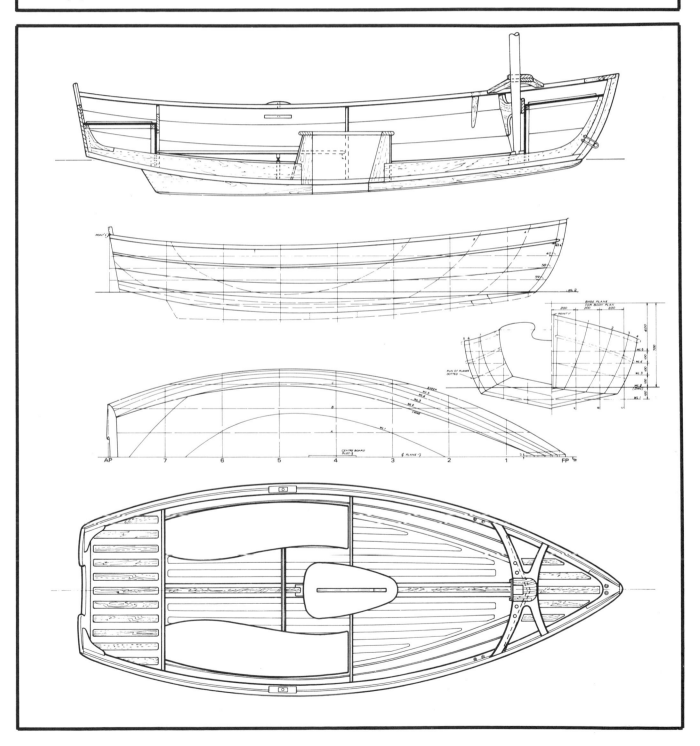

12'8" Catspaw Dinghy

by Herreshoff & White

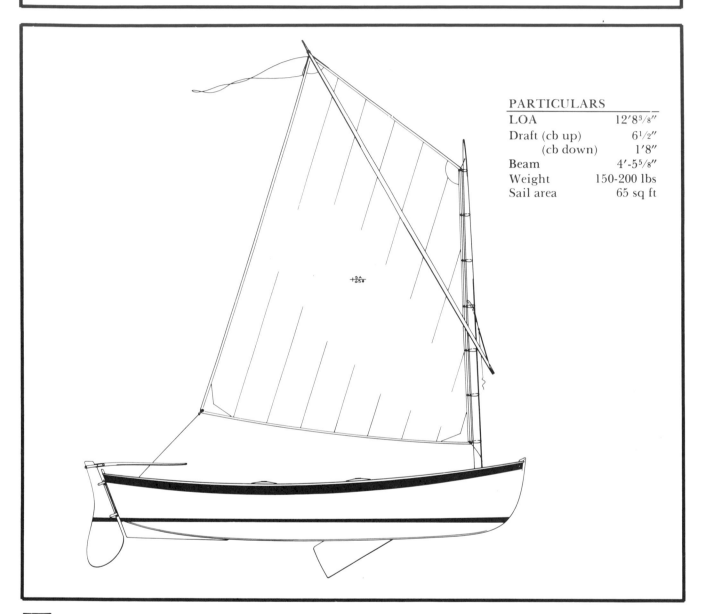

PARTICULARS

LOA	12'8³/₈"
Draft (cb up)	6¹/₂"
(cb down)	1'8"
Beam	4'-5⁵/₈"
Weight	150-200 lbs
Sail area	65 sq ft

These plans have evolved from some modifications made by Joel White and WoodenBoat on the design of a Herreshoff Columbia model lapstrake dinghy now in the collection of Mystic Seaport Museum. Plans for the original 11¹/₂' version were published in *Building the Herreshoff Dinghy* by Barry Thomas and were the basis for this 10% enlargement.

Because lapstrake boats are vulnerable to plank damage when used as beach boats on rocky Maine shores, it was decided to go to smooth-planked carvel construction, with the plank thickness increased from ³/₈" to ¹/₂". A pivoted centerboard was adapted so that the board could strike bottom without harm to itself or the trunk. A single boomless sprit rig gave the boat shorter spars and gave the crew less aggravation.

The plans for this boat are very detailed and include full-size mold patterns which, if used with the building instructions contained in WB Nos. 26, 27, and 28, should make this lovely round-bottomed boat easy to build for an amateur. Full-size patterns for the stem, transom, rudder, and station molds are included with the lines, offsets, construction plan, and sail plan. Lofting is not required. If one is determined to build a round-bottomed boat, this could make an ideal first one.

WoodenBoat's Catspaw Dinghy carries three people in comfort; more can be accommodated if conditions are calm. Two people can carry her for short distances, as in loading on a truck or trailer, or lifting up and down a beach. She's a good all-around boat, rows easily, sails well, and tracks well when towed. Although we are not enthusiastic about the idea, she could be powered by a small outboard. She is very seaworthy. WB Plan No. 12. $60.00.

Plan 12

DESCRIPTION

Hull type: Round-bottomed, transom stern, centerboarder

Rig: Spritsail

Construction: Carvel planked over steamed frames

PERFORMANCE

*Suitable for: Protected waters

*Intended capacity: 3-4

Trailerable: Yes

* *See page 112 for further information.*

Propulsion: Sails, oars, outboard

Speed (knots): 2-4

BUILDING DATA

Skill needed: Intermediate

Lofting required: No

*Alternative construction: Lapstrake or strip

Helpful WB issues: WB Nos. 26-28, or monograph

PLANS DATA

No. of sheets: 6

Level of detail: Extreme

Cost per set: $60.00

WB Plan No. 12

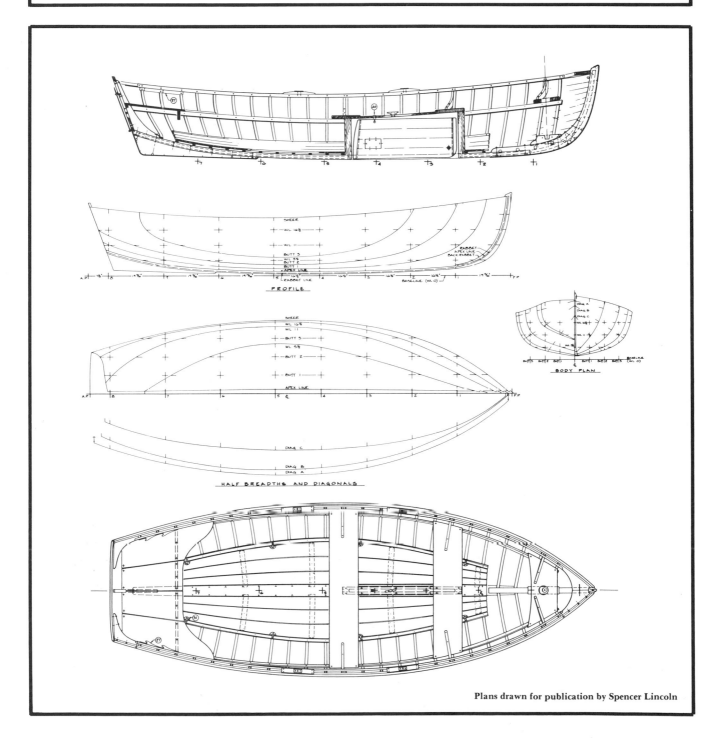

Plans drawn for publication by Spencer Lincoln

12'8" Sailing Canoe, Piccolo

by Robert H. Baker

PARTICULARS

LOA	12'8"
Beam	2'6"
Draft	8"
Weight	about 60 lbs
Sail area	52.3 sq ft

Piccolo was especially designed for WoodenBoat by Bob Baker—a man we feel had an unfailing eye for form and proportion and the firsthand experience with small boats that is needed to make them perform well.

So that she could carry two persons and be used with both sail and paddle, Piccolo was given a bit more beam and a few inches more freeboard than is usual for strictly double-paddle canoes. The need for light weight—thus easy cartopping—dictated that she be undecked. And so she would not dry out and leak after being in storage ashore, she was made lapstrake and given a white-painted bottom—the latter to reflect the sun's heat when bottom up.

Compared with most undecked sailing canoes, Piccolo is seaworthy—we've had her out in some brisk weather and she has never given us cause for concern. But that's relative to other boats of her type. Being only 12'8" long and undecked, she cannot be thought of as a craft that can survive in stormy conditions, and good judgment must come into play when using her. We feel she's at her best when sailing in the shelter of a harbor or river or when cruising near to shore.

Under sail, even with two people in her, she's a good performer. In spite of not having a centerboard (added weight and complexity) or a deep keel (which would keep her out of some good cruising ground), she doesn't slide sideways noticeably. She is slow in tacking, however, and has to be sailed around by playing with the sheets (or, of course, you can always cheat and use the paddle to get her across the eye of the wind).

As to her rig, designer Baker said, "You would hardly expect to get up and run around the boat to handle it, so it had to have everything led to within easy reach of one person. Her spars had to be kept short enough so they'd all stow comfortably inside the boat, yet I wanted a rig large enough to drive her along at a good speed—I wanted the boat to really sail, not just look like she might. The ketch rig seemed obvious from the start; you can get a reasonable amount of area in the two sails, spread out fore and aft to balance the deep ends of the hull and set low enough not to overpower her. The standing lug is ideal. Jam cleats are used so you can dump the whole rig in a hurry."

Piccolo's hull alone weighs just over 50 pounds—an indication of her delicacy. To build her and keep her from harm, one has to be a bit fussy. If you appreciate fine things, though, Piccolo is one of the finest we know.

Complete building instructions, written by her designer/builder, were published in WB Nos. 36 and 37. These plans include all the ones used in those articles, along with an extra drawing that details the spars and carrying yoke. WB Plan No. 20. $36.00.

Plan 20

DESCRIPTION
Hull type: Round-bottomed doubler-ender
Rig: Standing lug ketch
Construction: Lapstrake planking over steamed
      frames

PERFORMANCE
*Suitable for: Protected waters
*Intended capacity: 1-2
Trailerable: Yes
Propulsion: Double-paddle, sail

* *See page 112 for further information.*

Speed (knots):   2-4

BUILDING DATA
Skill needed: Intermediate
Lofting required: Yes
*Alternative construction: None
Featured as "How-to-Build" article in WB Nos.
      36 and 37

PLANS DATA
No. of sheets: 4
Level of detail: Above average
Cost per set: $36.00
WB Plan No. 20

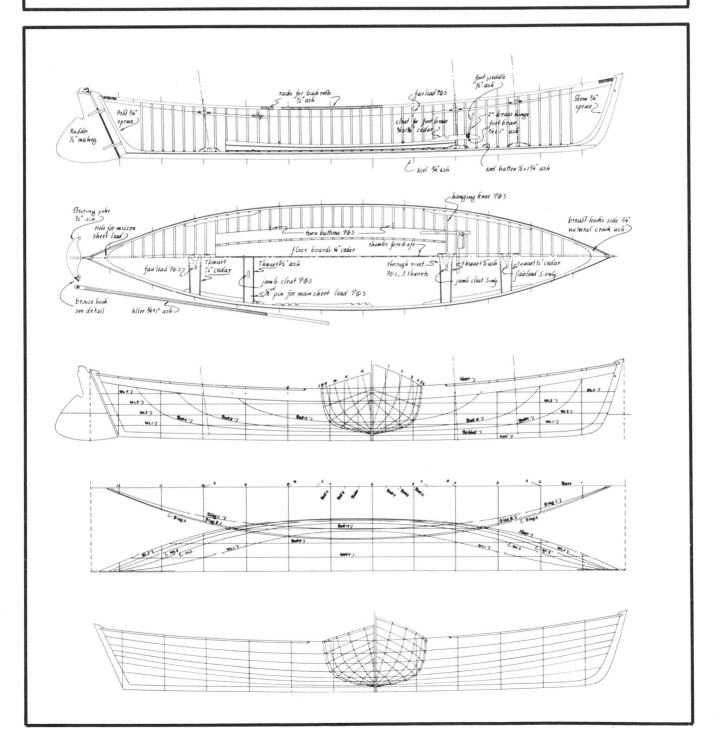

16' Double-Ended Pulling Boat, Shearwater

by Joel White

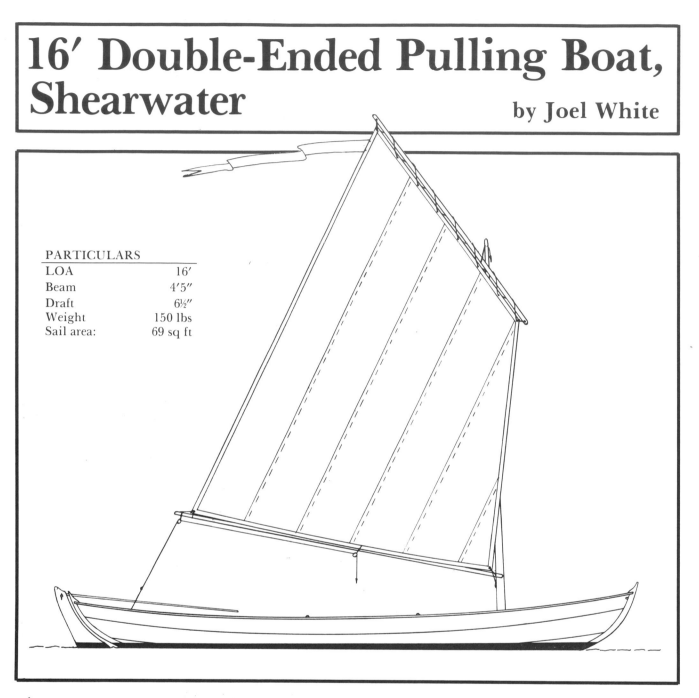

PARTICULARS

LOA	16'
Beam	4'5"
Draft	6½"
Weight	150 lbs
Sail area:	69 sq ft

Another in the series of lapstrake plywood small craft designed by Joel White especially for WoodenBoat, Shearwater combines the style of the wonderful open boats of western Norway and the performance of a Maine peapod with the ease of construction and durability of lapstrake plywood. She's narrow at the waterline, for a long, lean shape below that lets her glide through the water without fuss; yet, her topsides flare out to give lots of reserve stability and enough beam at the rail so that long oars can be used. Underwater, her bow and stern rise up so that she'll turn quite quickly under oars, and not trip on her forefoot to become a liability when towed as a tender behind a larger boat in a following sea.

Her hull, elegant and shapely as it is, is a study in simplicity, consisting of a backbone, three frames, and six planks—three to a side. Drawings for a sailing version are included, showing how to build the centerboard and trunk, rudder and tiller (she steers with a Norwegian-style cross-arm and push-pull tiller), and spars. We've found her to be

unusually fast under sail and great fun in moderate seas, but because of her speed under sail, her low freeboard, and undecked hull, she's not a sailboat for all weather. When it gets rough, she's drier and safer under oars at speeds slow enough for her to rise to meet the oncoming waves.

At 16' overall and 150 lbs, she's suitable for cartopping and, at the same time, suitable for carrying a sizeable load. Because she's of plywood, she won't dry out in the sun when not waterborne. And because her interior is uncluttered with the usual frames, chines, seat risers, and inwales, she's very easy to keep clean, to sand, and to paint. Her seats and floorboards are easily removed—they just lift out—making the task of caring for her even easier. There's no doubt about it, Shearwater is a wonderful combination of beauty, simplicity, versatility, and performance.

Plans come in eight sheets, and include sail plan, profile and oars plan, building jig details, construction plan, lines and offsets, plus three sheets of full-size patterns. WB Plan No. 58. $75.00.

Plan 58

DESCRIPTION
Hull type: Double-chined, V-bottomed
Rig: Single lugsail
Construction: Glued lapstrake plywood
PERFORMANCE
*Suitable for: Protected waters
*Intended capacity: 3-4
Trailerable: Yes

See page 112 for further information.

Propulsion: Oars and sail
Speed (knots):   2-4
BUILDING DATA:
Skill needed: Intermediate
Lofting required: No
*Alternative construction: None
PLANS DATA
No. of sheets: 8
Level of detail: Above average
Cost per set: $75.00
WB Plan No. 58

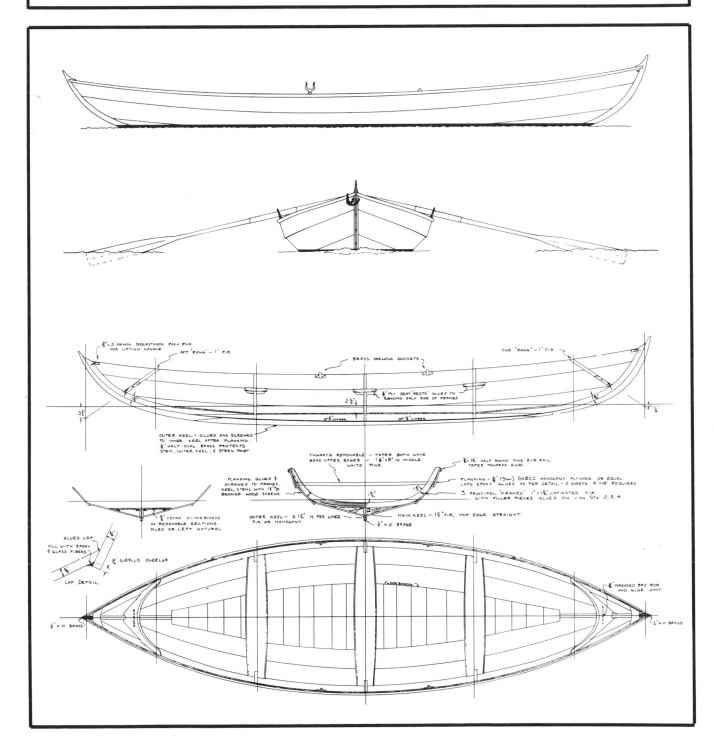

20' Rowing Wherry Bangor Packet

by Joel White

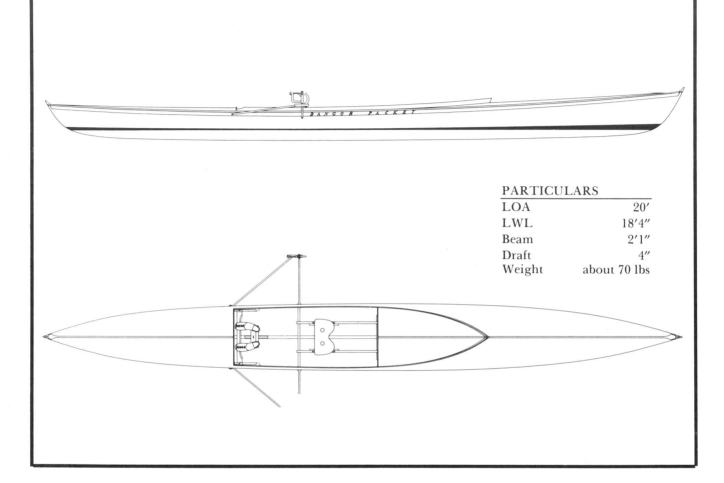

PARTICULARS

LOA	20'
LWL	18'4"
Beam	2'1"
Draft	4"
Weight	about 70 lbs

It's hard to find plans for a sliding-seat rowing craft that strikes a happy balance between an out-and-out high-performance craft and a traditional Whitehall-type pulling boat that has been fitted with small outriggers and a seat that slides. To fill this void WoodenBoat arranged with Joel White to sell the plans for such a "compromise" boat of his design—and it's indeed a beauty.

The Bangor Packet was designed with fun, exercise, and improved stability in mind—not to mention classic good looks. With a beam of 2', she is proportionally wider than the usual shell or single scull, giving her noticeably more stability and allowing the rower to sit lower down inside the boat, rather than on top of it. As you can judge for yourself from looking at the plans, she still has nice long lines for speed, yet with some flare to her sections up forward and a graceful sheer, she is both better-looking and more sea-worthy than the average competition boat.

Construction is cold-molded for light weight and strength. The hull is built upside down with three layers of 1/16" red-cedar veneer glued to each other over a building jig. The stems are of laminated strips of 1/8" Sitka spruce. A light plywood deck is fitted for seaworthiness, but is removable, being bedded rather than glued to the hull, and attached with oval-headed screws whose heads are left exposed. For cleaning and painting the interior every few years, you simply take off the deck. Weight of the finished hull is 55 pounds; the sliding seat and outrigger assemblies boost the total outfitted weight to about 70 pounds.

The first few boats were built over a trap-type jig made of the usual station molds with 3/4 x 1" pine ribbands let into them and spaced about 1 1/2" apart. This is still the easiest setup for building one or two boats, but it means that temporary staples have to be driven in abundance to hold each layer in place while the glue dries. A solid building form is now used; while this is more time-consuming to make, it allows vacuum bagging—of all three layers at one time and eliminates the need for most of the stapling. It greatly decreases the production time.

The 9'9" racing oars really move her along, and there is usually a waiting line at her builder's float to get aboard and try the fun. Being so close to the water, the feeling of speed is quite extraordinary.

The plans consist of five sheets, and include lines and offsets, outboard profile and deck plan, construction plan, and full-size loftings of stem and sternposts. WB Plan No. 36. $60.00.

Plan 36

DESCRIPTION
Hull type: Round-bottomed, double-ended
Construction: Cold-molded
Featured in Design Section: WB No. 52

PERFORMANCE
*Suitable for: Protected waters
*Intended capacity: 1

See page 112 for further information.

Propulsion: Oars
Speed (knots):   Up to 8

BUILDING DATA
Skill needed: Advanced
Lofting required: Yes
*Alternative construction: None

PLANS DATA
No. of sheets: 5
Level of detail: Above average
Cost per set: $60.00
WB Plan No. 36

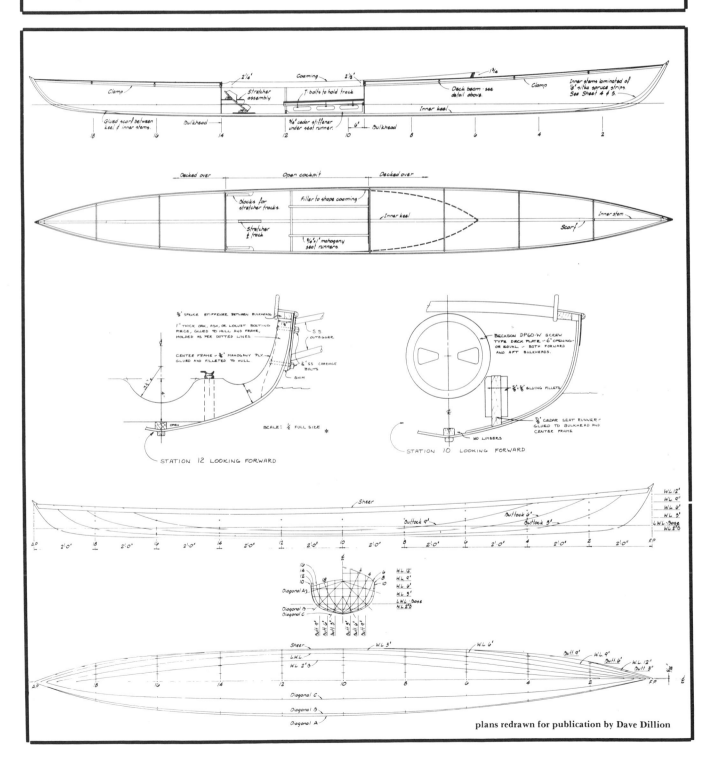

plans redrawn for publication by Dave Dillion

22'6" Recreational Shell Kingfisher

by Graeme King

PARTICULARS

LOA	22'6"
Beam	1'7"
Draft	4"
Weight	42 lbs

Those who know the sport of rowing know Graeme King to be one of the top designers and builders of wooden racing shells in the world today. The rowing shells that come out of his King Boat Works are built not only to stand the test of time, but have put their crew and the designer in the record books. The Harvard and Navy crews, as well as other outstanding crews, use King-designed boats.

Recognizing a strong resurgence in recreational rowing today, WoodenBoat commissioned King to design a single shell that the home builder would be capable of constructing. The result is Kingfisher, a graceful, V-bottomed shell that does not require a lot of expensive jig and mold making, and is very well suited to one-off construction by the amateur builder with intermediate boatbuilding skills.

Stability is a delicate matter in a shell, as any beginner discovers when he or she first settles onto the sliding seat! Kingfisher's 1'4" waterline beam provides a good compromise, giving inexperienced rowers a shell they can learn to handle, but also proving to be very satisfying to the experienced oarsman. She can be rowed in a variety of conditions, ranging from a glass-smooth river to a two-foot open-bay chop (only the oarsman very familiar with shells, of course, should try to row in anything but smooth water). The prototypes were thoroughly tested in two pulling boat races (which included a variety of other shell designs), one

on Narragansett Bay off Newport, and one in Boston Harbor in very rough conditions. The boat proved to be excellent to row on flat water, handled chop very well, and had a surprisingly fast turn of speed; she won both races handily. Intended as a recreational rather than all-out competition boat, Kingfisher can still reach an estimated 93% of the speed of the best competition shells.

Construction is of 3/32" or 1/8" mahogany plywood for the hull and bulkheads, with spruce stringers and a deck of shrunk Dacron. The boat is 22'6" overall, 1'7" beam, and has a 4" draft. With a weight of only 45 pounds, she may be readily transported to your rowing site on a car roof, and is easily carried by one person. A key to comfortable and efficient rowing is the rigging, as the designer knows very well, having formerly been rigger for the Harvard crews and the U.S. National teams.

The four sheets of plans include general arrangement, fitting details, bulkhead details and strongback, keel and patterns. WB Plan No. 51. $75.00.

A complete construction kit for the Kingfisher is also available from King Boat Works, and the kit comes with everything you need to build your boat, except varnish and oars. For those who are building from plans, outriggers and hardware can be purchased separately from King Boat Works as well. Write to WoodenBoat for details.

Plan 51

DESCRIPTION
Hull type: V-bottomed shell
Construction: Plywood planking over bulkhead-type frames

PERFORMANCE
*Suitable for: Protected waters, up to 12″ chop
*Intended capacity: 1
 Trailerable: Car-top
 Propulsion: Oars

See page 112 for further information.

Speed (knots):   Up to 10

BUILDING DATA:
Skill needed: Intermediate
Lofting required: No
*Alternative construction: None
"How to Build" instructions: WB Nos. 61 & 62, or monograph

PLANS DATA
No. of sheets: 4
Level of detail: Above average
Cost per set: $75.00
WB Plan No. 51

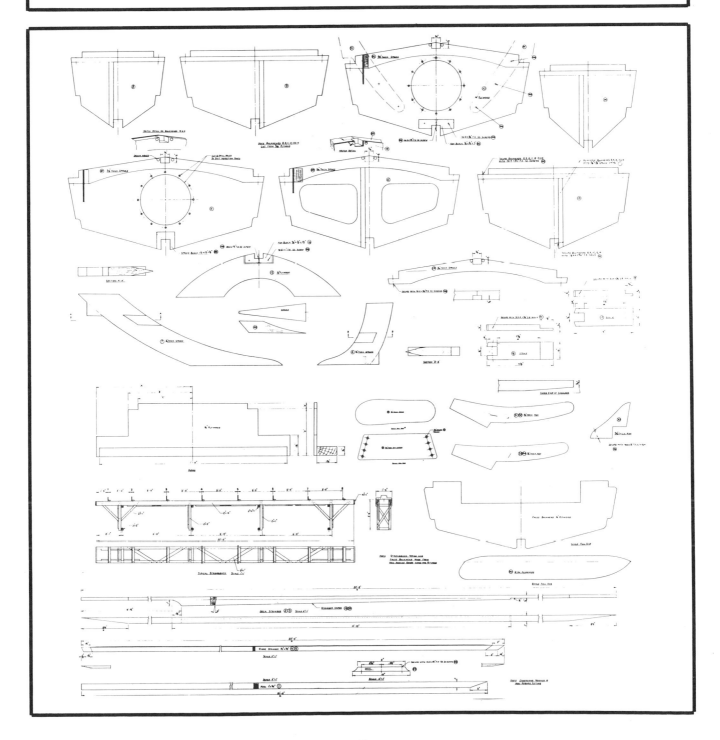

27' Round-Bottomed Single Shell "Best Boat" by Uffa Fox

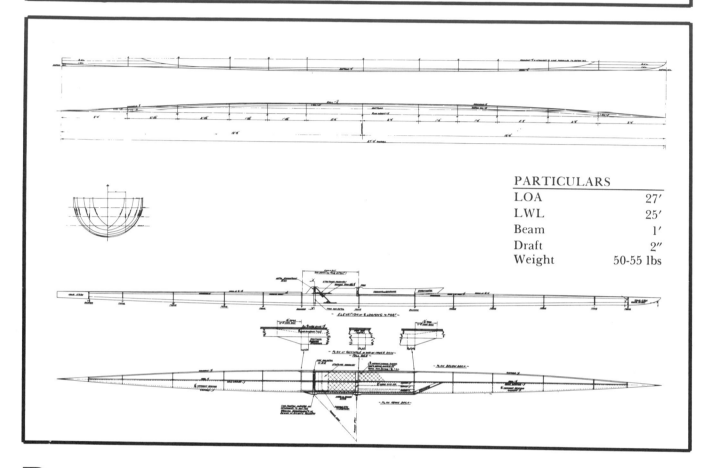

PARTICULARS

LOA	27'
LWL	25'
Beam	1'
Draft	2"
Weight	50-55 lbs

Designed in 1934, the Best Boat was what Uffa Fox considered his best rowing craft in terms of performance, lightness, and speed—the result of gradual improvement over the years by first-rate builders. When powered by a single rower in a sliding seat, both the original 27' round-bottomed version and the subsequent 26' V-bottomed version would travel at 10 knots, or double their natural speed*—with the "flowing motion of a thoroughbred," said Fox.

*The easily attained or natural speed of any displacement boat is a function of the square root of her waterline length.

The original round-bottomed Best Boat has circular midsections for the least wetted surface, and the long length that reduces wave-making to minimum. The shell is built of three layers of cold-molded plywood veneer, with double diagonal inner skins followed by a longitudinal outer skin. The solid stem and stern are designed to be easily removed in the event of damage.

The plans consist of three sheets—lines, offsets, and construction details. (See ‡ below.)

Plan 40

DESCRIPTION
Hull type: Round-bottomed shell
Construction: Cold-molded

PERFORMANCE
*Suitable for: Protected waters
*Intended capacity: 1
Propulsion: Oars

Speed (knots): Up to 10

BUILDING DATA
Skill needed: Advanced
Lofting required: No
*Alternative construction: None

PLANS DATA
No. of sheets: 3
Level of detail: Average

‡ Plans now available from Uffa Fox Ltd. Please inquire for address.

* See page 112 for further information.

26' V-Bottomed Single Shell "Best Boat" by Uffa Fox

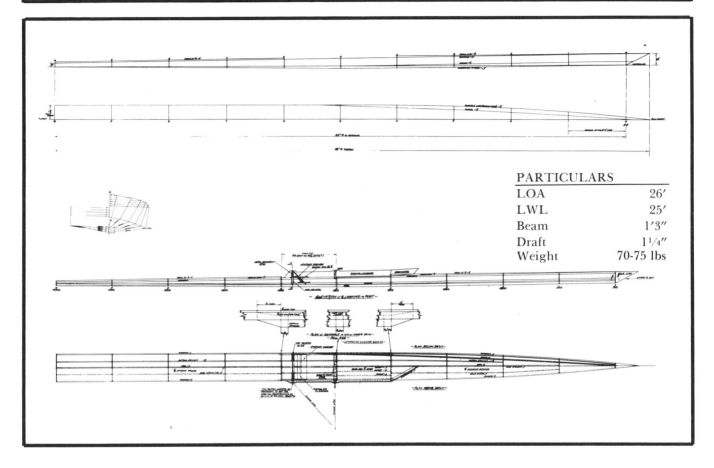

PARTICULARS	
LOA	26'
LWL	25'
Beam	1'3"
Draft	1¼"
Weight	70-75 lbs

This hard-chine plywood modification of the original round-bottomed Best Boat was designed by Uffa Fox in 1934. Although shorter (26' rather than 27') and somewhat beamier, this V-bottomed sliding-seat shell is just as fast as the original, traveling at up to 10 knots. Fox's motive in further improving his Best Boat design was to see if a semi-planing speed could be reached. Although the hull weight of the V-bottomed version had been reduced and the boat was somewhat easier to build, the speed remained the same. (See WB No. 54.)

The hull is built upside down over frames on a trestle, with two skins of plywood applied to the frames.

Plans are in three sheets, with lines, offsets, sections, and construction details. (See ‡ below.)

Plan 37

DESCRIPTION

Hull type: V-bottomed shell

Construction: Plywood planking over bulkhead-type frames

Featured in Design Section: WB No. 54

PERFORMANCE

*Suitable for: Protected waters

*Intended capacity: 1

* See page 112 for further information.

Propulsion: Oars

Speed (knots): Up to 10

BUILDING DATA

Skill needed: Intermediate

Lofting required: No

*Alternative construction: None

PLANS DATA

No. of sheets: 3

Level of detail: Average

‡ Plans now available from Uffa Fox Ltd. Please inquire for address.

21'3" Utility Launch

by Nelson Zimmer

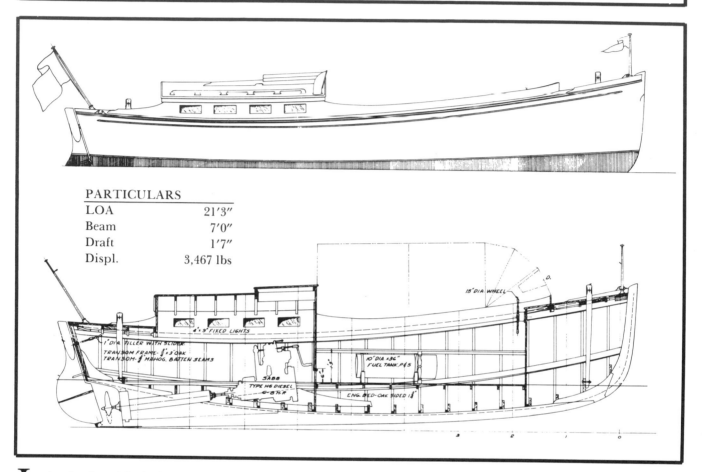

PARTICULARS

LOA	21'3"
Beam	7'0"
Draft	1'7"
Displ.	3,467 lbs

In developing this design, Nelson Zimmer tells us his inspiration came from the many slim, handsome launches and cruisers that silently and gracefully passed by his waterside home in the days following World War I. Then, three horsepower served an 18' launch admirably, and a 28' cruiser might have had a 15-hp Kermath beneath her bridge deck. Because these engines were by today's standards slow turning and low powered, they ran, if not silently, at least with a gentle, low-key rhythm that could even be called soothing.

But with the advent of power created by marine adaptation of the cheap, mass-produced, fast-turning automobile engine with its high (but sometimes questionable) power ratings, along with the blandishments of Madison Avenue and the stylists, the moderate launches and cruisers became obsolete in the eyes of most owners—but not extinct.

A case in point is the example shown. Designed as a tender to a Canadian north-woods fishing camp, her principal task is to ferry passengers and supplies between the camp and town, some miles across a rather large lake. Great speed was not desired; what was wanted was an able hull, one that could cope with the chop from a fresh breeze or glide silently through the water to avoid disturbing the fishing grounds.

In the interests of economy and the conservation of limited fuel supplies, the boat was designed to use the splendid little Sabb single-cylinder, 6- to 8-hp diesel, a true marine engine, remarkably free from the vibration that plagues most one-lungers.

Since this little launch is only 20' long on the waterline, it cannot be expected that she can be pushed much beyond 7 statute miles per hour, after which she will leave her stern wave behind and begin to squat, to the detriment of increased speed. But it should be noted that her top speed is achieved at about half throttle, when the standard 2:1 reduction gear gives a shaft speed of about 700 turns, providing plenty of torque to swing a big efficient wheel. At that rate, fuel consumption is a little under four-tenths of a U.S. gallon per hour, which translates to about 18 mpg—not bad, even from an automobilist's point of view.

This little 21x7' hull has a shape that is easy to frame and build, and her light scantlings make for economy of material. Backbone and framing is white oak, planking is cedar or mahogany, screw fastened or copper riveted.

The cuddy aft provides a safe place to stow gear and offers shelter against a passing rain squall or a chill breeze, while with the canvas hood indicated on the drawings and some camping equipment, she can even double as an overnight cruiser. All in all, a good, commonsense little boat.

Plans, consisting of four sheets, include lines, offsets, construction, and metalwork details. WB Plan No. 21. $105.00.

Plan 21

DESCRIPTION
Hull type: Round-bottomed
Construction: Carvel planked over steamed frames
Featured in Design Section: WB No. 43

PERFORMANCE
*Suitable for: Somewhat protected waters
*Intended capacity: 6-8 day running, 2 cruising
Trailerable: With difficulty

See page 112 for further information.

Propulsion: 6- to 8-hp single-cylinder diesel
Speed (knots):   Up to 7

BUILDING DATA
Skill needed: Advanced
Lofting required: Yes
*Alternative construction: Cold-molded, strip

PLANS DATA
No. of sheets: 4
Level of detail: Average
Cost per set: $105.00
WB Plan No. 21

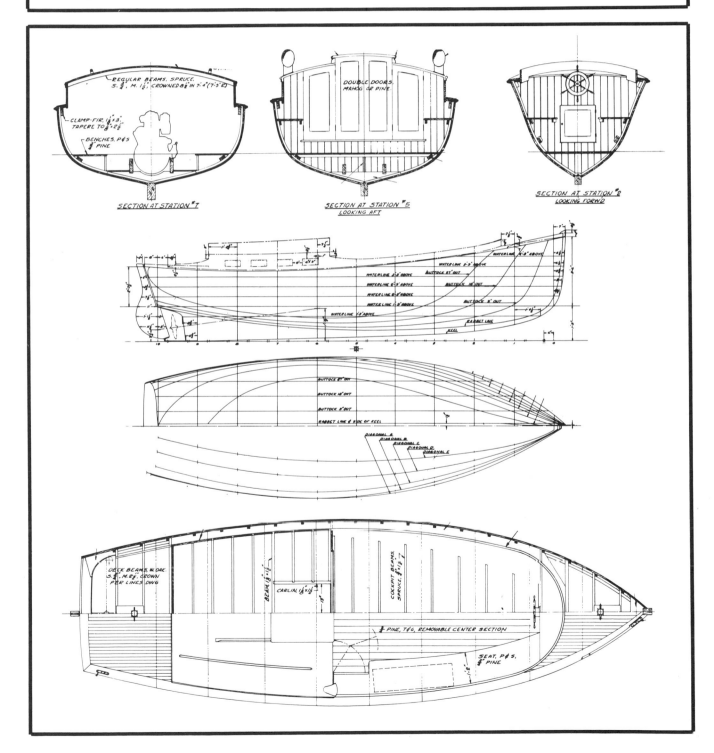

25' Bassboat

by Eldredge-McInnis

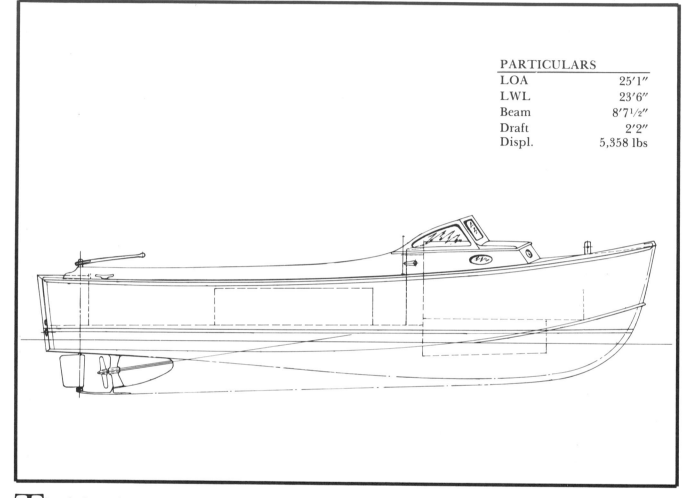

PARTICULARS	
LOA	25'1"
LWL	23'6"
Beam	8'7½"
Draft	2'2"
Displ.	5,358 lbs

The design of powerboats has been a specialty of Eldredge-McInnis ever since 1928, when the firm started in business, and since then hundreds of successful power craft designs have been produced. Considering the firm's experience and proximity to Buzzards Bay—thus having firsthand knowledge about the notoriously choppy water there—it's little wonder that 50 or 60 bassboats have been built to Eldredge-McInnis designs since 1951, when the first one came out. A 24' hull was chosen initially, as being short enough for quick handling from either of her two tiller-operated steering stations, yet long enough to span a Buzzards Bay wave. Later on, the design was enlarged a bit for more room in the cabin; this (at the designer's recommendation) is the version sold by *WoodenBoat*. Still later, a 26' model was developed.

Fishing for striped bass was their first calling and the reason for the name; however, these boats have proven themselves as yacht club launches, workboats, and commuters. Planing with the recommended 6-cylinder, 350-cubic-inch engine and not too heavily loaded, these bassboats will do 20 knots or so and give you a dry and comfortable ride, but they drive well at the lower, non-planing speeds as well—a feature not found in modern deep-V hulls generally

designed only for high-speed operation. This bassboat hull has the beam and stability to deal with off-center loading; the boat won't heel badly even if several people crowd to one side. A full-length spray rail helps keep the passengers dry, and the self-bailing cockpit drains off the rainwater and any spray that might come aboard while running.

This is primarily a day boat with emphasis on a big usable cockpit surrounding the oversize 6'-long engine box in which boat gear as well as the engine can live, and on which one can sit or recline. However, there is room below in the cabin for a toilet, a settee, and a basic galley, making limited cruising in this bassboat a possibility.

There are two framing setups shown for building the hull. For amateurs, the sawn-frame version would be easiest and best; you simply build the frames, set them in position, and build the boat around them. Alternately she can be built using steam-bent web frames, resulting in a somewhat stronger boat.

If going fast, keeping dry, and riding in comfort are high on your list, this could be the boat for you.

Plans come in six sheets, including outboard profile, lines and offsets, construction plans, and both sawn and web frame sections. WB Plan No. 52. $150.00.

Plan 52

DESCRIPTION
Hull type: V-bottomed
Construction: Carvel planked over sawn frames
Headroom/cabin (between beams): About 4'6"

PERFORMANCE
*Suitable for: Somewhat protected, yet choppy, waters
*Intended capacity: 2-8 day cruising

* See page 112 for further information.

Trailerable: With difficulty; permit required
Propulsion: 300-350 cu in inboard
Speed (knots): 10-20

BUILDING DATA:
Skill needed: Advanced
Lofting required: Yes
*Alternative construction: Strip

PLANS DATA
No. of sheets: 6
Level of detail: Above average
Cost per set: $150.00
WB Plan No. 52

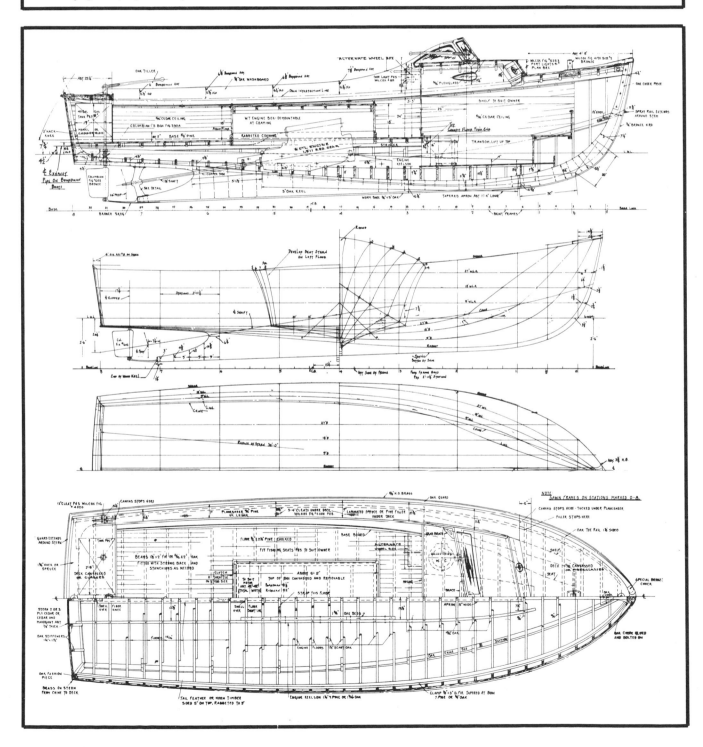

32' Power Cruiser

by Eldredge-McInnis

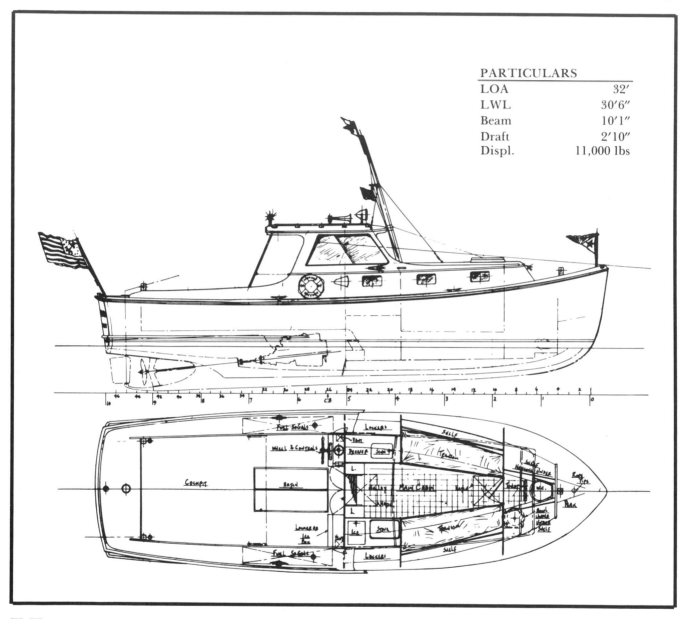

PARTICULARS

LOA	32'
LWL	30'6"
Beam	10'1"
Draft	2'10"
Displ.	11,000 lbs

Here is a power cruiser developed from the much-admired Maine lobsterboat by one of the all-time great powerboat designers. She'll do nearly 20 knots with a single engine of 300 horsepower; there's loads of room in her big self-bailing cockpit; there's full headroom in both her cabin and steering shelter; and she's lovely to look at. There's little in the way of rough water this boat can't handle, and with her generous freeboard and high flaring bow, not much spray will ever come aboard.

The emphasis here is on lots of room outside in the cockpit, yet for two people there's ample room in the cabin for comfortable cruising. Upper and lower berths to starboard are shown on one plan, giving a big galley opposite and a spacious enclosed head forward, but there are several other possibilities—V-berths forward, galley and head

opposite each other aft, for example. There is adequate space in the cabin to install whatever arrangement suits you best.

The hull is "built down" somewhat; that is, it has been designed with hollow down near the keel toward the stern—a feature that adds considerable strength. This hull will be stronger than a hull whose backbone lies mostly outside the planking rabbet.

Building this boat would be quite an undertaking for a lone amateur, so you would do well to hire at least some professional help. But when finished, there's no doubt that this 32' cruiser would be well worth the effort and expense.

The plans consist of five sheets, including profile and arrangement, lines and offsets, inboard construction, cabin plans, and construction section. WB Plan No. 53. $150.00.

Plan 53

DESCRIPTION
Hull type: Round-bottomed lobsterboat type
Construction: Carvel planked over steamed frames
Headroom/cabin (between beams):   About 6'

PERFORMANCE
*Suitable for: Open ocean
*Intended capacity: 4-6 day running, 2 cruising
Trailerable: With difficulty; permit required

* *See page 112 for further information.*

Propulsion: 300-hp single-screw gas or diesel
Speed (knots):   18-19

BUILDING DATA:
Skill needed: Advanced
Lofting required: Yes
*Alternative construction: Strip or cold-molded

PLANS DATA
No. of sheets: 5
Level of detail: Above average
Cost per set: $150.00
WB Plan No. 53

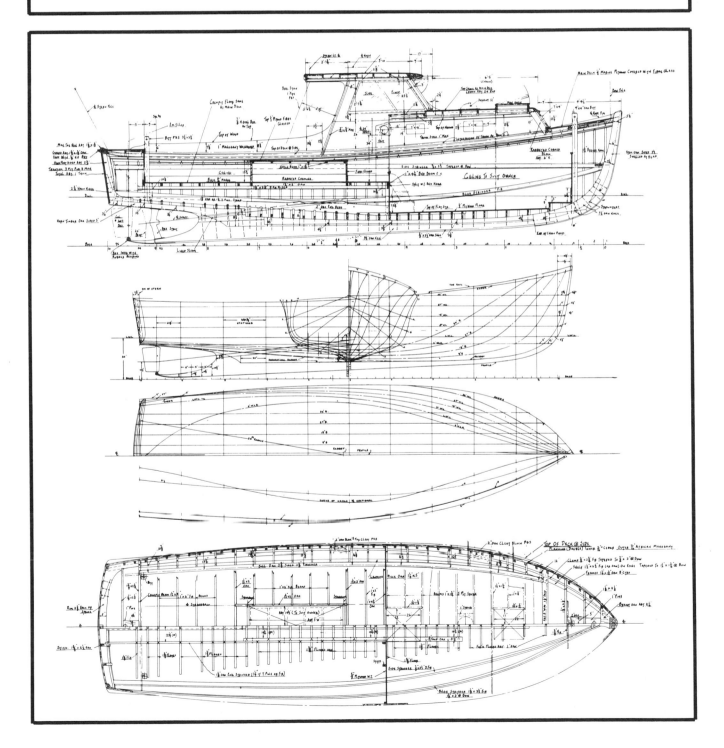

14'11" Plywood Catboat

by Charles Wittholz

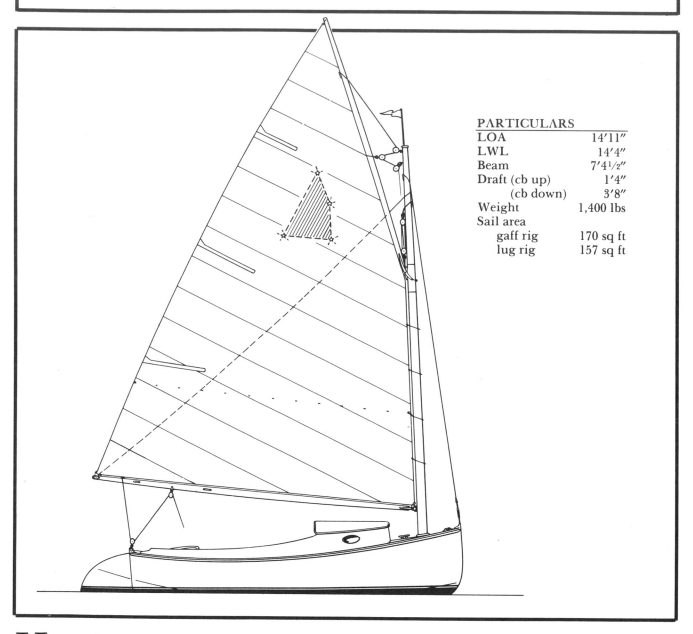

PARTICULARS	
LOA	14'11"
LWL	14'4"
Beam	7'4½"
Draft (cb up)	1'4"
(cb down)	3'8"
Weight	1,400 lbs
Sail area	
gaff rig	170 sq ft
lug rig	157 sq ft

Here is an easily built small boat with a big heart. A seaworthy daysailer or vest-pocket cruiser, Corvus (named for the constellation known to mariners as the "gaff-rigged mainsail") has the look of a traditional Cape Cod catboat with tumblehome stem, a beam of almost half her length, and a "barn-door" rudder on her stern. She has room for six adults in her 7'-long cockpit, and there's a "head" in her small cabin. Some builders have extended the trunk cabin a bit in order to fit in two berths for cruising. A few other boats have been built without any cabins at all for use as open daysailers. For auxiliary power, a small outboard can be mounted on the stern, or an inboard engine can be installed. (There's information on one of the drawings for this latter option.)

Corvus is designed for planking with ³/₈" plywood over eight sawn frames. She's well thought out for amateur construction; the plans contain better-than-average detail and even show how to fit Corvus with an outside ballast keel, if you'd prefer that over a centerboard. While her designer recommends the conventional gaff mainsail, there is an alternate lug rig shown having a considerably shorter mast—a special requirement for one boat that had to pass underneath a bridge on her way to open water.

These boats make delightful daysailers because they sail at a small angle of heel, and the centerboard version can be used where the water is but knee-deep.

Plans come in seven sheets, including sail plans, spar and rigging details, lines and offsets, construction plan, keel construction details, inboard profile and arrangement. WB Plan No. 47. $75.00.

Plan 47

DESCRIPTION
Hull type: V-bottomed, centerboard boat
Rig: Cat
Construction: Plywood planking over sawn frames
Headroom/cabin: approx. 3'6"

PERFORMANCE
* Suitable for: Protected waters
* Intended capacity: 2-6 daysailing

Trailerable: Yes
Propulsion: Sails, oar, engine
Speed (knots): 2-4

BUILDING DATA
Skill needed: Intermediate
Lofting required: Yes
*Alternative construction: None

PLANS DATA
No. of sheets: 7
Level of detail: Above average
Cost per set: $75.00
WB Plan No. 47

See page 112 for further information.

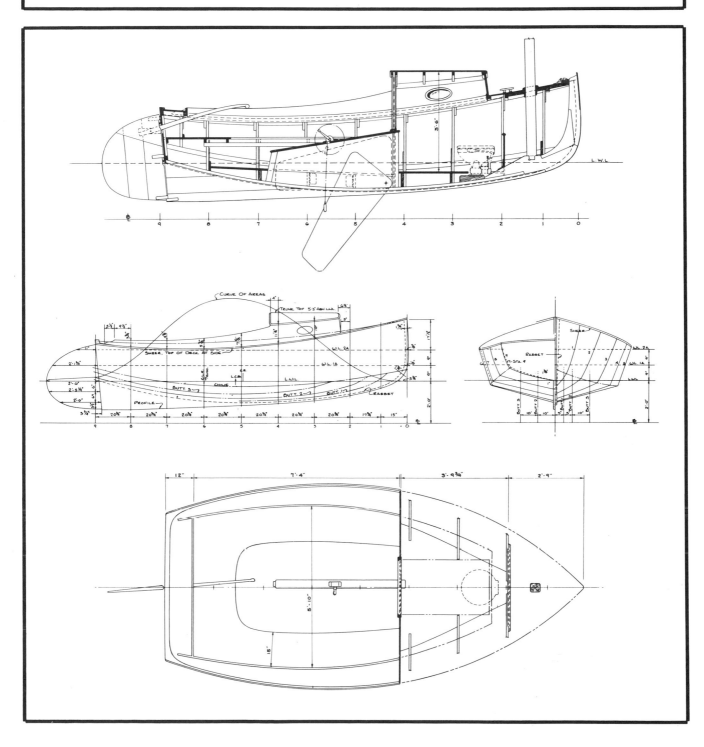

16' Centerboard Sloop Lively

by Uffa Fox

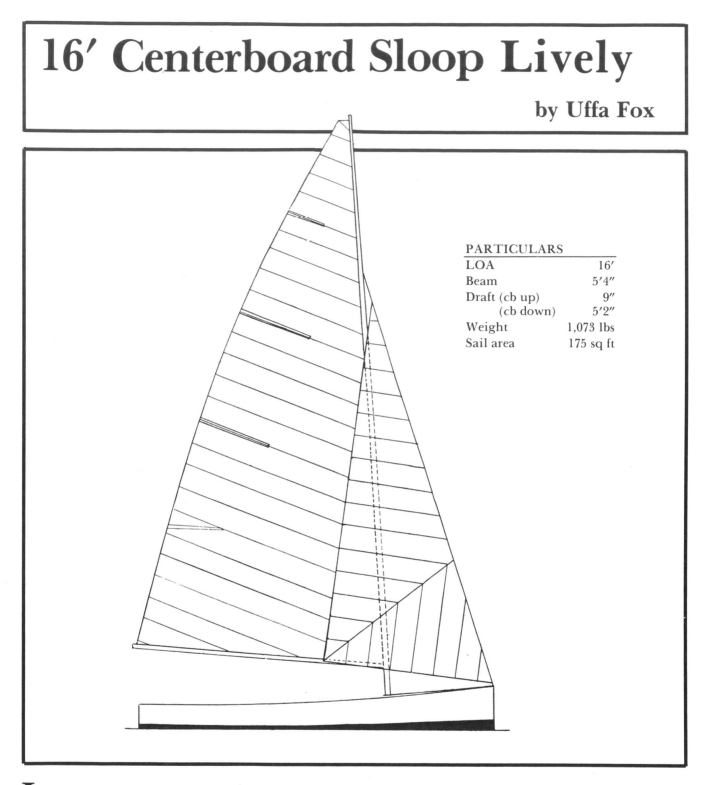

PARTICULARS

LOA	16'
Beam	5'4"
Draft (cb up)	9"
(cb down)	5'2"
Weight	1,073 lbs
Sail area	175 sq ft

Lively, a classic thoroughbred, was designed by the great Uffa Fox as a new one-design class for Britain's North Norfolk Sailing Club in 1938. She was intended for racing with a crew of three adults, in shallow water, and to withstand trailering on bumpy roads. She has a drop rudder and a lead-ballasted centerboard, with a long centerboard case that forms a kind of central girder, and adds great strength to her hull. Lively as her name and fast in light air, she planes at high speed in fresh breezes, yet is easily handled in hard weather. Lively was Norfolk's fastest 16-footer in the 1938 season, and she delighted Fox with her responsiveness.

Her interesting construction calls for 1/16" diagonal inner planking, with a 3/16" outer fore-and-aft skin fastened to 1/4 x 3/8" frames spaced 2" apart, giving her a light but very strong hull—albeit a complex one. She has wide side decks which are comfortable to sit upon since the coamings have been kept low. Being a spirited light-displacement boat, there is no need for an after deck, and the absence of one allows easy access to the rudder.

Lively's rig is quite modern-looking and very efficient, with its tall marconi mainsail and moderately overlapping jib. It should move the boat along well in all winds, yet be easily handled at all times.

Plans consist of four sheets, including lines and offsets, construction plan, sail plan, and spar details. WB Plan No. 45. $45.00.

Plan 45

DESCRIPTION
Hull type: Round-bottomed centerboarder
Rig: Marconi sloop
Construction: Double-diagonal planking over
   steamed frames

PERFORMANCE
*Suitable for: Protected waters
*Intended capacity: 1-3

* *See page 112 for further information.*

Trailerable: Yes
Propulsion: Sail
Speed (knots):   3-6, up to 12 planing

BUILDING DATA
Skill needed: Advanced
Lofting required: Yes
*Alternative construction: Cold-molded

PLANS DATA
No. of sheets: 4
Level of detail: Average
Cost per set: $45.00
WB Plan No. 45

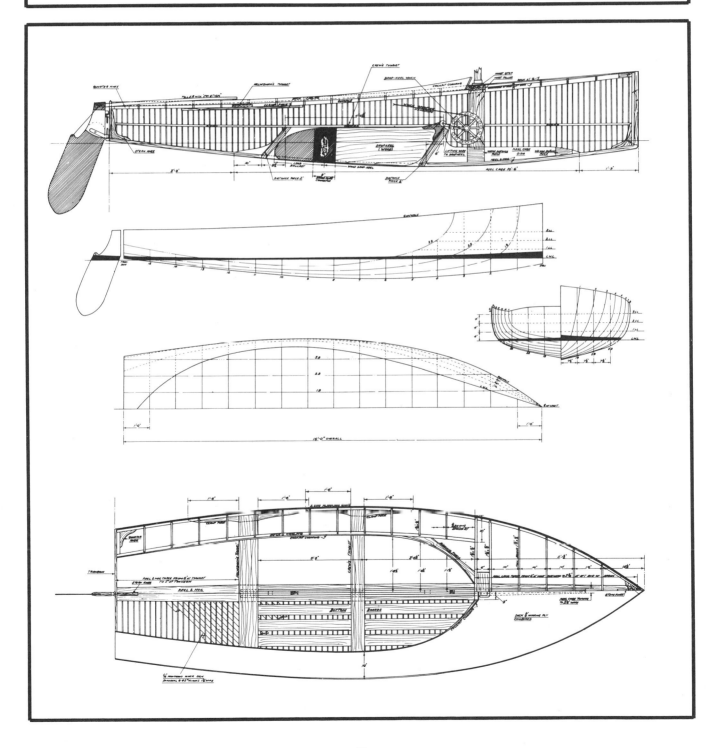

18'3" Sloop, O-Boat

by John G. Alden

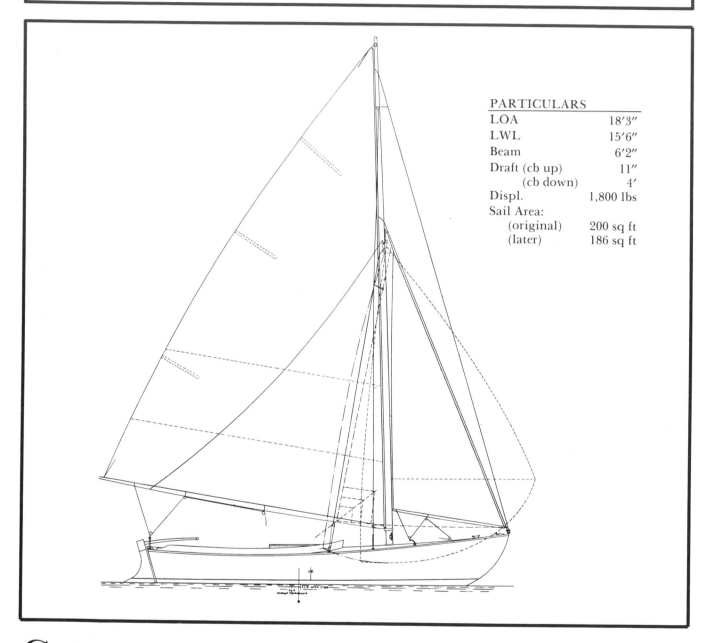

PARTICULARS	
LOA	18'3"
LWL	15'6"
Beam	6'2"
Draft (cb up)	11"
(cb down)	4'
Displ.	1,800 lbs
Sail Area:	
(original)	200 sq ft
(later)	186 sq ft

Created out of a desire to provide young sailors with able boats of their own at a reasonable price, the O-boats as a class were created in 1921. The class was to provide a different kind of training than that available through the more common method of developing skill and experience as crew aboard the fast-but-wet racing machines of the time. So the men at John Alden's rallied to produce something with generous freeboard (especially forward), plenty of beam, and a deep cockpit. A bulkhead forward of the mast creates a watertight compartment, and the boats are said to be unsinkable as a result.

They were extremely successful boats, incorporated into the fleets of many yacht clubs from Maine to New York, and appearing in fleets as far away as Honolulu.

Basically, two boats were developed to roughly the same lines. This original was a bit longer and slightly less beamy than the modified version, but both versions were rather widely accepted according to individual preferences. Some yacht clubs or individuals even had Alden develop versions with more radical modifications, such as the Thousand Islands One-Designs, which were simply 15' O-boats.

They turn up all the time, these days, and are as suited to their original purpose as ever. With their versatile centerboard configuration they can go nearly anywhere, but they're able enough by reputation to stand up to the weather and water of more open bays as well.

The plans include lines, offsets, construction, two sail plans, and specifications. WB Plan No. 6. $90.00.

Plan 6

DESCRIPTION
Hull type: Round-bottomed centerboard boat
Rig: Marconi sloop
Construction: Carvel planked over steamed frames
Featured in Design Section: WB No. 42

PERFORMANCE
*Suitable for: Protected bays
*Intended capacity: 3-6 daysailing

Trailerable: Yes
Propulsion: Sail
Speed (knots): 3-5

BUILDING DATA:
Skill needed: Intermediate to advanced
Lofting required: Yes
*Alternative construction: Cold-molded, strip

PLANS DATA
No. of sheets: 4
Level of detail: Average
Cost per set: $90.00
WB Plan No. 6

See page 112 for further information.

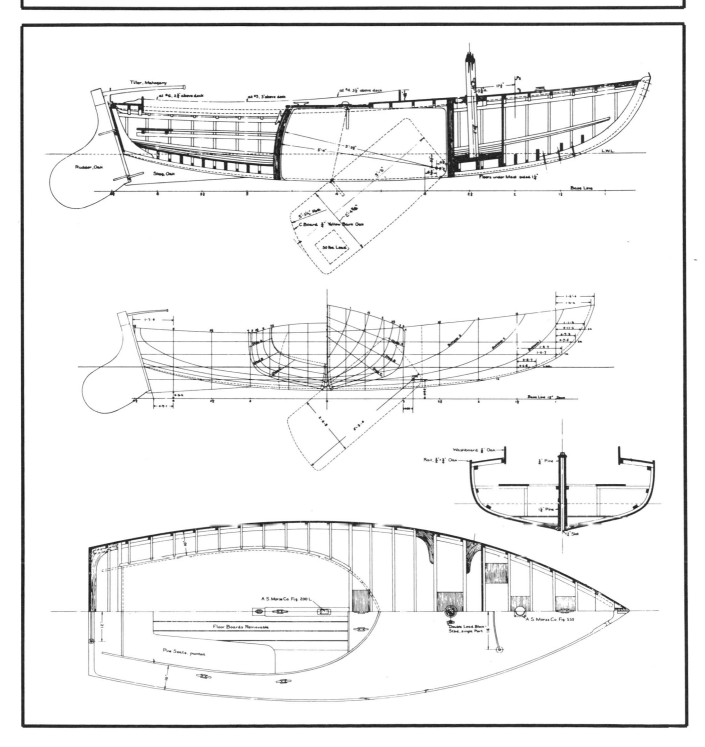

18'8" Mackinaw Boat

by Nelson Zimmer

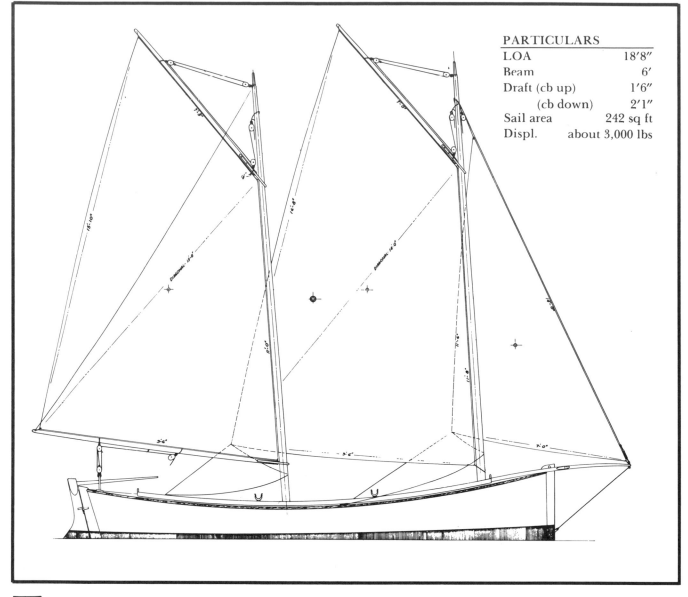

PARTICULARS	
LOA	18'8"
Beam	6'
Draft (cb up)	1'6"
(cb down)	2'1"
Sail area	242 sq ft
Displ.	about 3,000 lbs

This boat is an historically accurate 18' version of the well-known, reputed Mackinaw boat, a sailing and rowing shallop type that was popular on Lakes Michigan and Superior in the late 1800s. The originals, which ran 26' or more, were known for their speed and seakeeping abilities, and this smaller version should exhibit many of the same endearing qualities.

Designed by Nelson Zimmer, the Mackinaw Boat has a LOA of 18'8", a 6' beam, and draws 1'6" with her centerboard raised. Her shoal draft will enable her to poke about in shallow waters and ground out at her mooring at low tide without trouble.

Her spars and gear are simple and inexpensive. An unusual detail is the main and mizzen halyards' arrangement, combining peak and throat into one line for each sail. Oars serve as auxiliary power. Being long-keeled, she won't tack very quickly, but with the right breeze, she'll provide a good turn of speed. This roomy, shoal-draft boat will give a good account of herself in a broad range of wind and sea conditions, and with a variety of loads. She could be trailered, or simply hauled up on the beach for winter.

The plans for the Mackinaw Boat show good detail, and an experienced amateur or a professional would be able to build her. Although she is best suited for carvel planking, some similar boats have been built lapstrake. We recommend white cedar and oak, but red cedar, yellow cedar, or western fir would be alternative choices. The denser woods such as hard mahogany should be avoided.

Further information is available in WB No. 45, in No. 23 in the "Tidings" and "Designs" sections, and in Howard Chapelle's *American Small Sailing Craft*. (This last reference is for the original.) WB Plan No. 14. $60.00.

Plan 14

DESCRIPTION
Hull type: Round-bottomed double-ender
    with centerboard
Rig: Gaff ketch
Construction: Carvel planked over steamed frames
Featured in Design Section: WB No. 23

PERFORMANCE
*Suitable for: Somewhat protected waters
*Intended capacity: 3-5

*See page 112 for further information.

Trailerable: Yes
Propulsion: Sail, oars, outboard
Speed (knots):   3-5

BUILDING DATA
Skill needed: Intermediate to advanced
Lofting required: Yes
*Alternative construction: Lapstrake, strip, or cold-
    molded

PLANS DATA
No. of sheets: 3
Level of detail: Average
Cost per set: $60.00
WB Plan No. 14

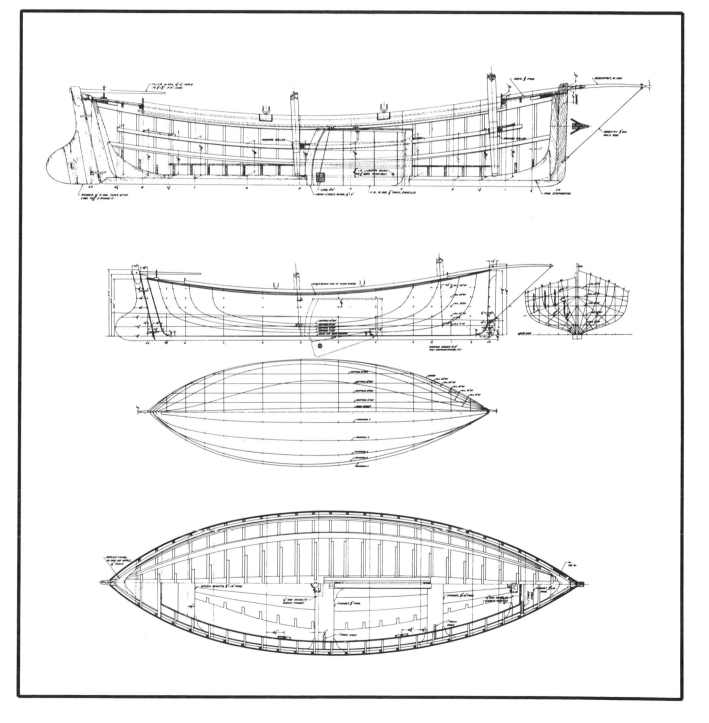

20'2" Sloop, Dark Harbor 12¹/₂
by B.B. Crowninshield

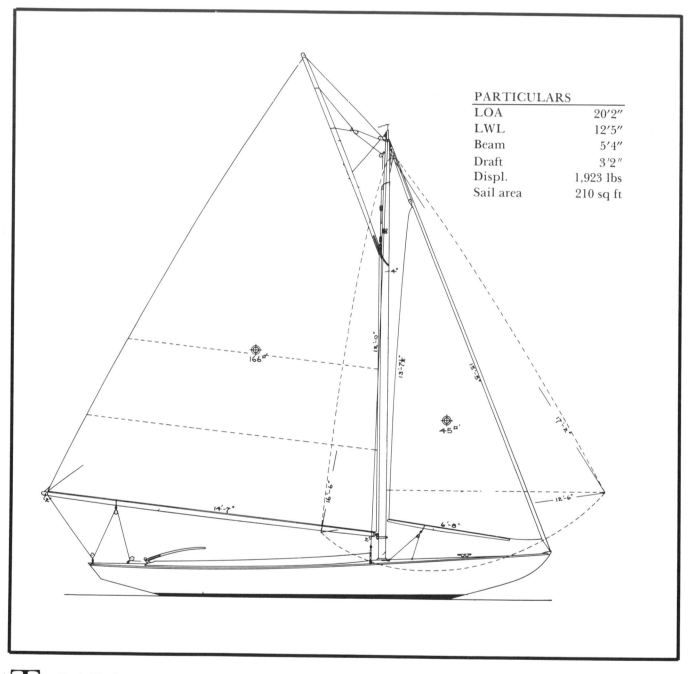

PARTICULARS

LOA	20'2"
LWL	12'5"
Beam	5'4"
Draft	3'2"
Displ.	1,923 lbs
Sail area	210 sq ft

The Dark Harbor 12½ keel sloop is a smaller, more easily handled but equally exciting version of the Dark Harbor 17½, without a cabin. This gaff-rigged daysailer, which was first built in 1915 and originally known as the Islesboro Class, is still active in racing from the Buck's Harbor Yacht Club in South Brooksville, Maine.

Like the 17½, The Dark Harbor 12½ is great fun to sail, can be easily handled by one, and moves along briskly in light air. She'll respond quickly, and with her outside ballast keel and self-bailing cockpit, can take as much rough weather as her crew can.

Construction of the Dark Harbor 12½, like that of her bigger sister, calls for a lead ballast keel, carvel planking over steamed oak frames, fastenings of copper rivets and bronze bolts, and a canvas-over-cedar-or-pine deck. The 12½'s size makes her considerably lighter and less expensive to build than the larger class.

Through an agreement with the Peabody Museum of Salem, Massachusetts, which now owns the original Crowninshield tracings, WoodenBoat has made these plans available. They consist of four sheets—lines, offsets, sail plan, and construction plan. WB Plan No. 18. $60.00.

Plan 18

DESCRIPTION

Hull type: Round-bottomed with outside ballast keel

Rig: Gaff sloop

Construction: Carvel planked over steamed frames

Featured in Design Section: WB No. 37

PERFORMANCE

*Suitable for: Somewhat protected waters

*Intended capacity: 2-4 daysailing

* *See page 112 for further information.*

Trailerable: With difficulty

Propulsion: Sail

Speed (knots):   3-5

BUILDING DATA

Skill needed: Advanced

Lofting required: Yes

*Alternative construction: Cold-molded, strip

PLANS DATA

No. of sheets: 4

Level of detail: Average

Cost per set: $60.00

WB Plan No. 18

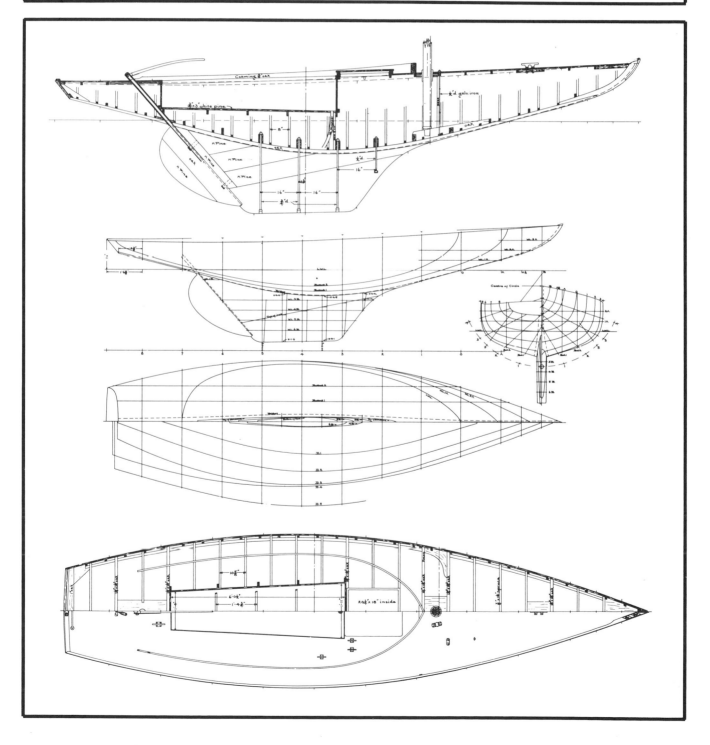

21'2" Sloop, Indian Class

by John G. Alden

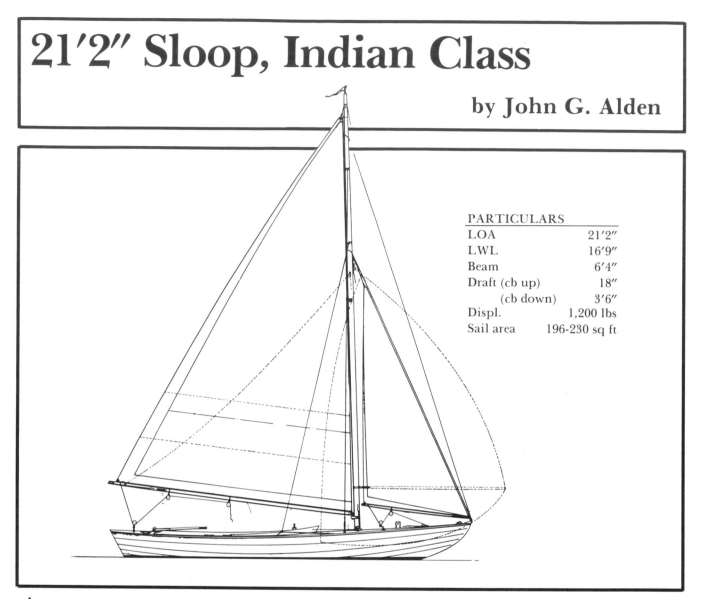

PARTICULARS	
LOA	21'2"
LWL	16'9"
Beam	6'4"
Draft (cb up)	18"
(cb down)	3'6"
Displ.	1,200 lbs
Sail area	196-230 sq ft

As the refinements of the Swampscott dory type reached its zenith, the need arose to depart more distinctly from the workboat origins—where rowing was as important as sailing—and to develop a dory type specifically for sailing in interclub races. And, as John Alden never failed to appreciate the trends of his time, he set Sam Crocker, then in his employ, to work on a sailing dory one-design class in early 1921. The result was a beautifully modeled 21-footer with a marconi rig, which carried 350 pounds of inside ballast.

The advantages of the new design over the traditional Swampscott were greater beam and firmer bilges, brought aft to the transom, which afforded the opportunity to carry more sail and thus perform better (on a triangular course). With its generous side decks and inside ballast, the design provided a margin of safety without diminishing the excitement factor. It was, in fact, a boat well suited to clubs with limited budgets and many young sailors.

William Chamberlain built the first boats (and many of the rest), which were sailed that year at Marblehead's Eastern Yacht Club. So successful were the boats that other clubs ordered more built, and the Indian class was well on its way.

In an age of high-performance planing craft, the Indian class has little to offer today's racing sailor, but before it vanishes into obscurity, we ought to take another look. It is, after all, a fine performer itself, and one that will sail well in all sorts of conditions. Given its relative simplicity of con-struction, it should be comparatively inexpensive to build.

The Indian is built dory-style, with the bottom, stem, transom, and six sawn frames being set up first. After the planking is completed, four pairs of steam-bent frames are set in place between each pair of sawn frames, the combina-tion providing a light, stiff hull. Because of that construc-tion, full lofting is unnecessary and dimensions can be picked up from the plan. An interesting option offered in the design is the so-called V-stern, wherein the garboard and broadstrake lap together at the transom without a knuckle, affording, presumably, somewhat less drag at this point.

The round-sided dory types require a wider-than-usual garboard, which can be very difficult to find these days. There are, of course, a number of ways of creating one wide plank from two narrow ones, but the cheapest and simplest solution might be to join them with typical riveted dory laps, perhaps made flush so as not to show. For the best guidance on dory history and construction, John Gardner's *Dory Book* (available from WoodenBoat Books) is un-matched.

The sheets include two different sail plans; one with 196 square feet and one with 230 square feet, lines (with offsets), construction plan, and a set of building specifications. Armed with these sheets, a builder with some experience should be able to produce an Indian class sloop and make a good job of it. Price for the set is $75.

Plan 5

DESCRIPTION
Hull type: Round-sided dory type
Rig: Marconi sloop
Construction: Lapstrake over sawn frames
Featured in Design Section: WB No. 42

PERFORMANCE
*Suitable for: Protected bays
*Intended capacity: 3-6 daysailing

* See page 112 for further information.

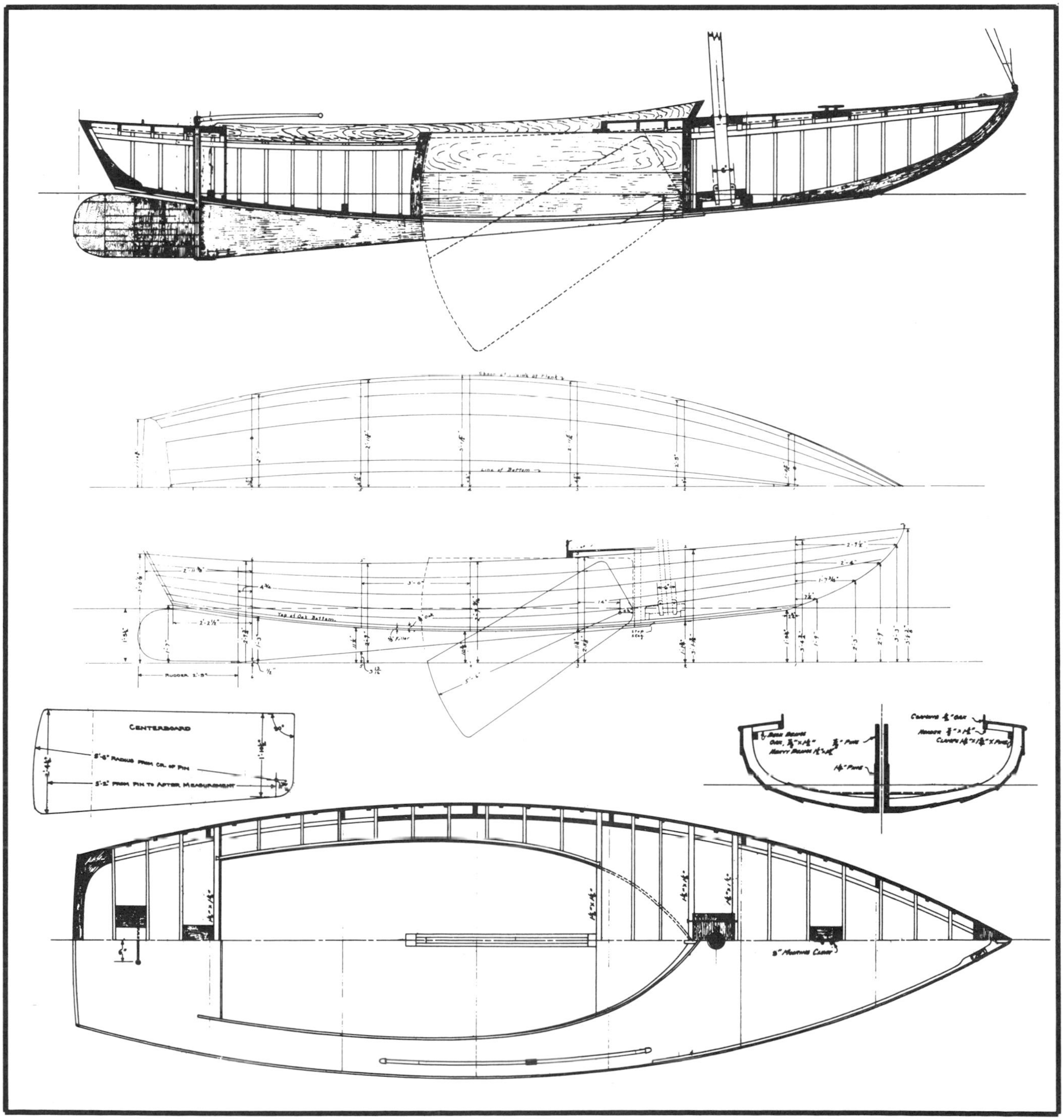

Trailerable: Yes
Propulsion: Sail
Speed (knots): 3-5

BUILDING DATA:
Skill needed: Intermediate to advanced
Lofting required: Partial
*Alternative construction: None

PLANS DATA
No. of sheets: 4
Level of detail: Average
Cost per set: $75.00
WB Plan No. 5

21'4" Hodgdon 21 Class Sloop

by George I. Hodgdon, Jr.

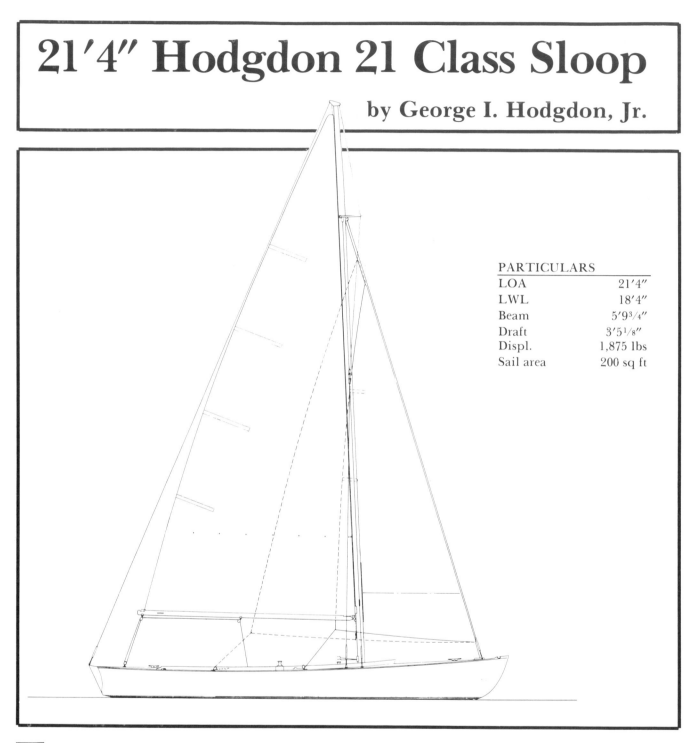

PARTICULARS	
LOA	21'4"
LWL	18'4"
Beam	5'9¾"
Draft	3'5⅛"
Displ.	1,875 lbs
Sail area	200 sq ft

The Hodgdon 21s are so stunningly beautiful that you never forget the shape once you've seen an actual boat. From every vantage point, afloat or ashore, it's an exquisite thing to behold. Her every line seems to curve and blend, giving the hull a sculpted appearance; even the ballast keel flows gracefully into the rest of her. And the boats sail as well as they look. They're fast, comfortable, weatherly, and comparatively dry.

Starting in 1958 with a model his uncle Charles had developed about 20 years earlier and from which a couple of successful boats had been built, George I. (Sonny) Hodgdon, Jr., added some refinements he'd picked up from his long and close association with L. Francis Herreshoff and Starling Burgess, plus some ideas of his own, to come up with this most beautiful of keel daysailers.

She carries an up-to-date and easily handled, aluminum-sparred marconi rig for which the hull has been especially reinforced—an extra long mast step, metal stirrups between the chainplates and that step, and a structural shelf at the deck edge in way of the chainplates. Her hull is nevertheless very light, weighing in at only about 875 pounds—considerably less than the weight of her lead ballast keel.

When you sail one of these boats, you sit comfortably sprawled on the cockpit platform, out of the wind, with the tiller right in your lap. There's no need to hike out on the deck or rail because, with her heavy keel, she has ample stability without the need of help from the weight of her crew.

The nine sheets of plans include sail plan, lines, offsets, keel construction, lead keel drawing, construction sections, deck framing, rudderstock and bow chock details. WB Plan No. 61. $90.00.

Plan 61

DESCRIPTION
Hull type: Round-bottomed, outside-ballasted keel boat

Rig: Marconi sloop

Construction: Carvel planked over steamed frames

PERFORMANCE
*Suitable for: Somewhat protected waters

*Intended capacity: 3-6 daysailing

See page 112 for further information.

Trailerable: With difficulty

Propulsion: Sail

Speed (knots): 3-6

BUILDING DATA:
Skill needed: Advanced

Lofting required: Yes

*Alternative construction: Cold-molded, strip

PLANS DATA
No. of sheets: 9

Level of detail: Average

Cost per set: $90.00

WB Plan No. 61

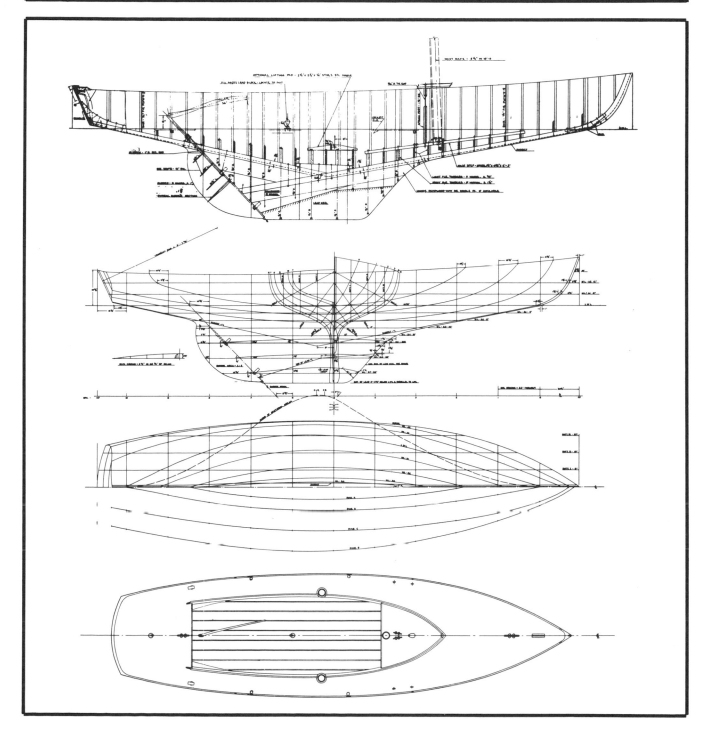

25'10" Sloop, Dark Harbor 17½

by B.B. Crowninshield

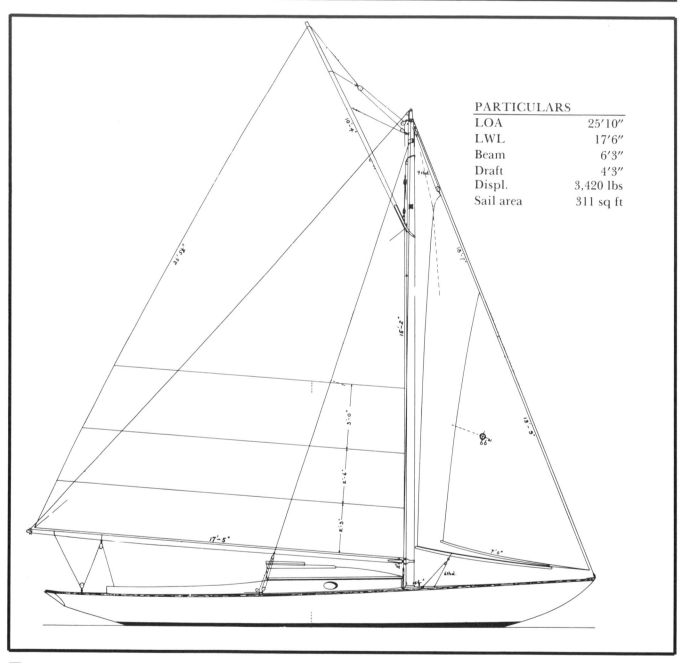

PARTICULARS	
LOA	25'10"
LWL	17'6"
Beam	6'3"
Draft	4'3"
Displ.	3,420 lbs
Sail area	311 sq ft

In 1908 B.B. Crowninshield was asked to draw up a one-design class of knockabouts to be initially known as the Manchester 17½. The class was to become one of the most popular and long-lived of the knockabouts; about 200 boats were built in Maine, for example, where the name was altered to reflect yacht club affiliation. The most common name for the design is now the Dark Harbor 17½, named after the summer colony at Islesboro that once had the largest number of these boats.

One still finds many a Dark Harbor 17½ "knocking about" New England waters. (A dozen or so reside at Buck's Harbor Yacht Club in Brooksville, where they are still raced on Eggemoggin Reach.) The boats were built well and have lasted well, with cedar planking over oak frames, a lead ballast keel, copper and bronze fastenings, and simple deck construction—canvas-over-cedar-or-pine—to discourage freshwater leaks. Most were built with the self-bailing cockpit as shown on the drawings, although a few were given deep cockpits with seats for more comfort.

While intended primarily for afternoon sailing and racing, these boats have often been used for coastal cruising; the low cabin trunk has space for two transom berths.

The plans consist of four sheets, including lines, offsets, sail plan, and construction plan. WB Plan No. 19. $60.00.

Plan 19

DESCRIPTION

Hull type: Round-bottomed with outside ballast keel

Rig: Gaff sloop

Construction: Carvel planked over steamed frames

Headroom/cabin (between beams): About 3'6"

Featured in Design Section: WB No. 37

PERFORMANCE

*Suitable for: Somewhat protected waters

* *See page 112 for further information.*

*Intended capacity: 4-6 daysailing, 2 cruising

Trailerable: With difficulty

Propulsion: Sail

Speed (knots): 3-6

BUILDING DATA

Skill needed: Advanced

Lofting required: Yes

*Alternative construction: Cold-molded, strip

PLANS DATA

No. of sheets: 4

Level of detail: Average

Cost per set: $60.00

WB Plan No. 19

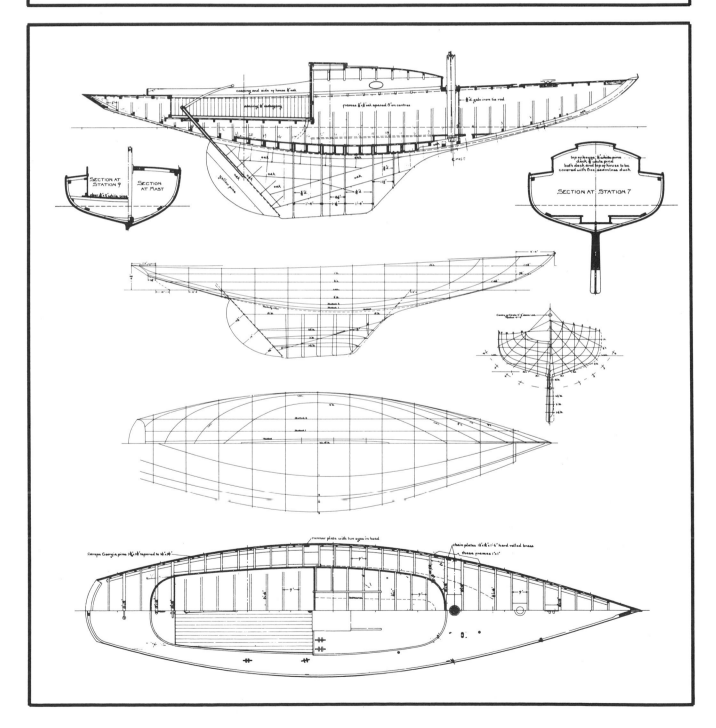

28'3" Camden Class Sloop

by B.B. Crowninshield

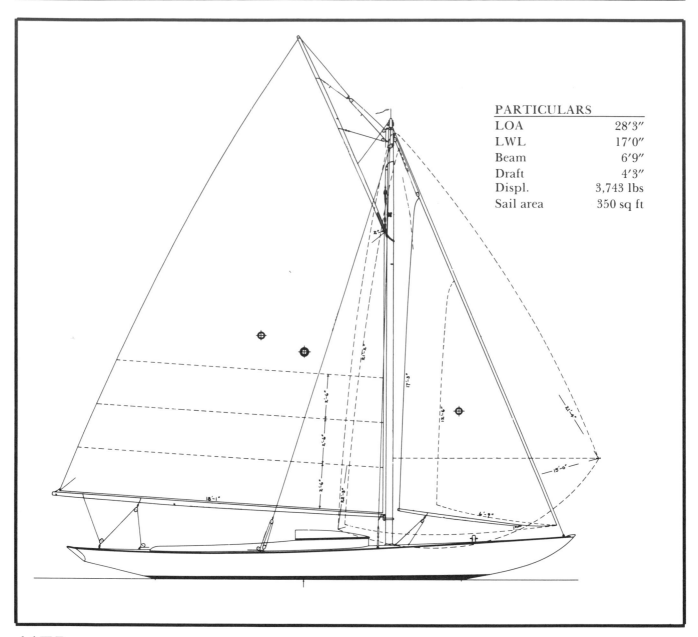

PARTICULARS	
LOA	28'3"
LWL	17'0"
Beam	6'9"
Draft	4'3"
Displ.	3,743 lbs
Sail area	350 sq ft

"Knockabout" was the popular turn-of-the-century name given to this type of fin-keeled jib-and-mainsail cabin sloop, up to about 30' long. These little day boat/racer/cruisers flourished before World War I and were found to be sensible craft, easily handled by one or two persons, fun to sail, and relatively inexpensive to build.

The 28'3" overall Camden Class day boat is longer ended, and perhaps better looking, than the other two Crowninshield knockabout designs (the Dark Harbor 12½ and 17½). She was designed in 1915 for the Camden (Maine) Yacht Club, and four boats were built by the Hodgdon Brothers yard in East Boothbay. At least one of these original boats survives as perhaps the finest combination of performance and beauty ever developed within the definitions of the design.

This gaff-rigged sloop has a simple, low trunk cabin, and is built primarily for daysailing and racing—although, with room for two small transom berths, she can be used for short cruises. As in the other two designs, construction calls for carvel planking over steamed frames, but the hull could alternatively be cold-molded or strip-planked. The fin keel is of lead-ballasted oak, and there are two watertight bulkheads.

The Camden Class sloop would certainly be a delight to sail, at her best in light winds, but able to hold her own in rough weather.

The four sheets of plans include lines, offsets, sail plan, and construction plan. WB Plan No. 17. $60.00.

Plan 17

DESCRIPTION

Hull type: Round-bottomed with outside ballast keel

Rig: Gaff sloop

Construction: Carvel planked over steamed frames

Headroom/cabin (between beams): about 3'6"

Featured in Design Section: WB No. 37

PERFORMANCE

*Suitable for: Somewhat protected waters

* See page 112 for further information.

*Intended capacity: 4-6 daysailing, 2 cruising

Trailerable: With difficulty

Propulsion: Sail

Speed (knots): 3-6

BUILDING DATA

Skill needed: Advanced

Lofting required: Yes

*Alternative construction: Cold-molded, strip

PLANS DATA

No. of sheets: 4

Level of detail: Average

Cost per set: $60.00

WB Plan No. 17

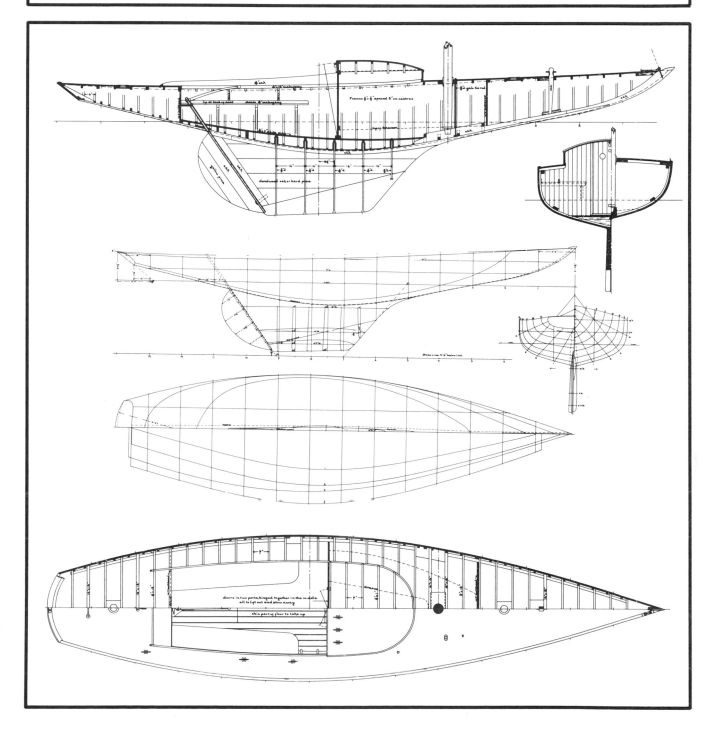

17'1" Plywood Catboat

by Charles Wittholz

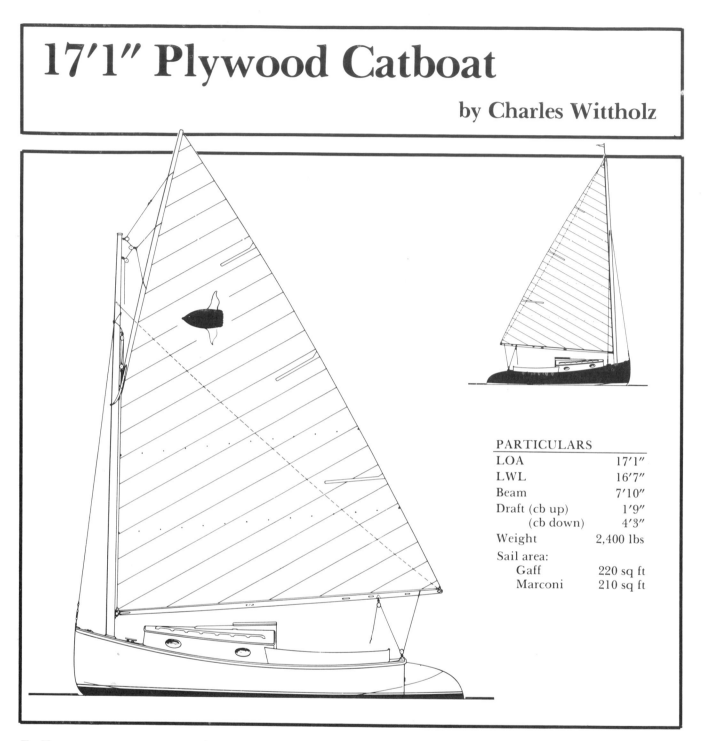

PARTICULARS	
LOA	17'1"
LWL	16'7"
Beam	7'10"
Draft (cb up)	1'9"
(cb down)	4'3"
Weight	2,400 lbs
Sail area:	
Gaff	220 sq ft
Marconi	210 sq ft

No doubt about it, a catboat has more room for her length than almost any other boat. And here is about the smallest possible catboat you'll find with real cruising accommodations for two. Inside her cabin, there's sitting headroom above her two V-berths and a toilet between them, a stove aft on one side, and a sink and icebox aft on the other. Still, her cockpit is huge—six or seven adults can be comfortably seated for daysailing. If you're most interested in seaworthiness, build the version with the self-bailing cockpit which, incidentally, has a big hatch for stowing the outboard auxiliary; if it's shelter and a backrest you're after, there's a deep cockpit option.

Options, in fact, abound on these drawings. There's a plan for a fixed outside ballast keel rather than a centerboard; there are drawings for a rabbeted mahogany wale strake at the sheer, a plan for an anchor-handling bowsprit,

and one for the installation of an inboard engine. You can fit her with either of the two rigs that are shown—gaff or marconi.

Like her smaller sister, Corvus, this 17-footer is designed to be easily and efficiently built. She is set up on her nine sawn frames, then planked and decked with 3/8" plywood. She's also designed with trailering in mind—her beam was kept under the 8' limit, she won't dry out in the sun and then leak when you launch her, and she's very easy to rig and get underway. She'd be a wonderful boat for taking overland to distant waters.

Plans come in 11 sheets, including outboard profile, sail plan (with spar and rigging details and bowsprit arrangement), lines and offsets (with or without mahogany sheerstrake), construction, keel construction details and plan for open cockpit model. WB Plan No. 48. $90.00.

Plan 48

DESCRIPTION
Hull type: V-bottomed, centerboard (optional keel)
Rig: Gaff or marconi cat
Construction: Plywood planking over sawn frames
Headroom/cabin (between beams): About 4'
PERFORMANCE
*Suitable for: Somewhat protected waters
*Intended capacity: 2-7 daysailing, 2 cruising

* See page 112 for further information.

Trailerable: Yes
Propulsion: Sail w/auxiliary
Speed (knots): 2-5
BUILDING DATA:
Skill needed: Intermediate
Lofting required: Yes
*Alternative construction: None
PLANS DATA
No. of sheets: 11
Level of detail: Above average
Cost per set: $90.00
WB Plan No. 48

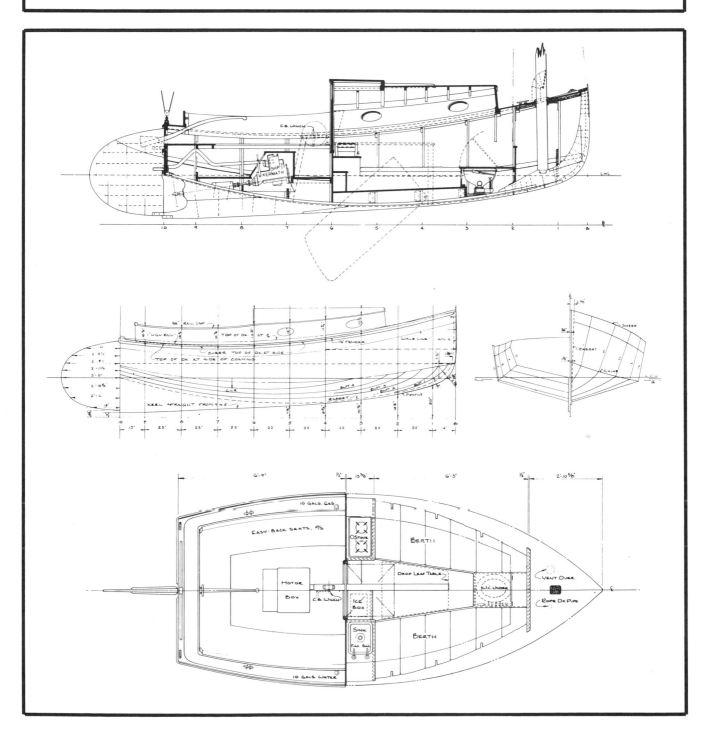

18' Catboat

by Fenwick Williams

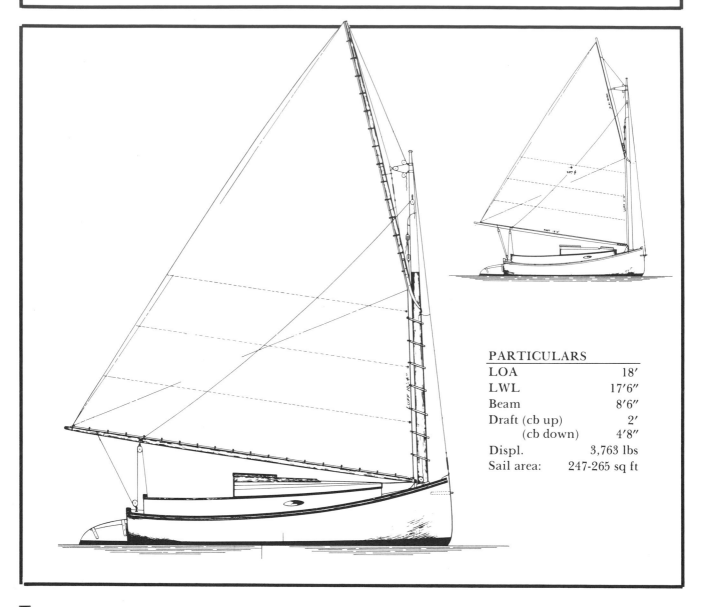

PARTICULARS	
LOA	18'
LWL	17'6"
Beam	8'6"
Draft (cb up)	2'
(cb down)	4'8"
Displ.	3,763 lbs
Sail area:	247-265 sq ft

If your taste runs more to the traditional, and if your building skills are correspondingly more advanced, this 18-footer by Fenwick Williams might be worth considering. She's only slightly larger than the Wittholz catboat (WB Plan No. 48) and has about the same cabin arrangement; however, her hull is carvel planked and round bilged—shaped just like the old-time cats that Cape Cod builders were noted for.

Williams, who first drew this boat in 1931 for himself and has added to and improved her since, had the amateur builder very much in mind. The drawings show a sawn frame at every station; these take the place of, and save having to build the usual temporary hull molds. Added later, in between each pair of these sawn station frames, are a couple of conventional steam-bent frames. To eliminate steam-bending elsewhere, the cabin sides and coamings are shown with corner posts, perhaps giving a less graceful

appearance than the traditional oval shape, but making those assemblies easier to build.

The original sail area was 247 sq ft, and if you want her rigged conservatively this is probably the best size. In later modifications, Williams increased the sail area a little; there are sail plans for both 257 sq ft and 265 sq ft. There are also drawings for a shorter oval-shaped cabin with matching oval coaming, an outside ballast keel, conventional all-bent frames, and an inboard engine.

This beautiful and traditional Cape Cod catboat from the dean of catboat designers, with her shallow draft, stiffness under sail, and overall roominess, could be just the cruiser you're looking for.

The set of plans comes in 11 sheets including: four sail plans, lines, offsets, construction, outboard profile, cabin construction and sections, and keel model. WB Plan No. 56. $125.00.

Plan 56

DESCRIPTION

Hull type: Round-bottomed, centerboard catboat w/optional keel

Rig: Gaff cat

Construction: Carvel planked over sawn and steamed frames

Headroom/cabin (between beams):   About 4'

PERFORMANCE

*Suitable for: Somewhat protected waters

*Intended capacity: 4-6 daysailing, 2 cruising

*See page 112 for further information.

Trailerable: Yes; permit required

Propulsion: Sail w/auxiliary

Speed (knots):   2-6

BUILDING DATA:

Skill needed: Advanced

Lofting required: Yes

*Alternative construction: Cold-molded, strip

PLANS DATA

No. of sheets: 11

Level of detail: Above average

Cost per set: $125.00

WB Plan No. 56

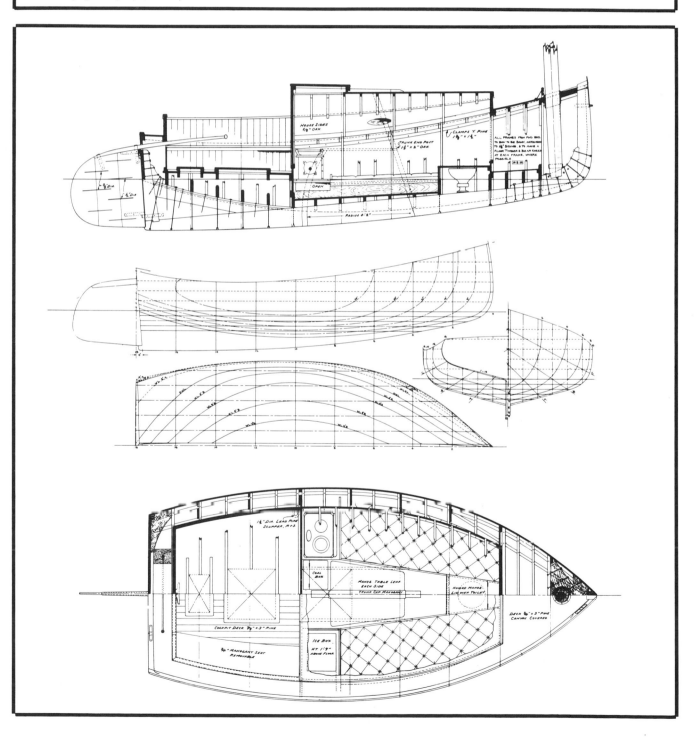

20'3" Sloop, Little Gull

by Winthrop Warner

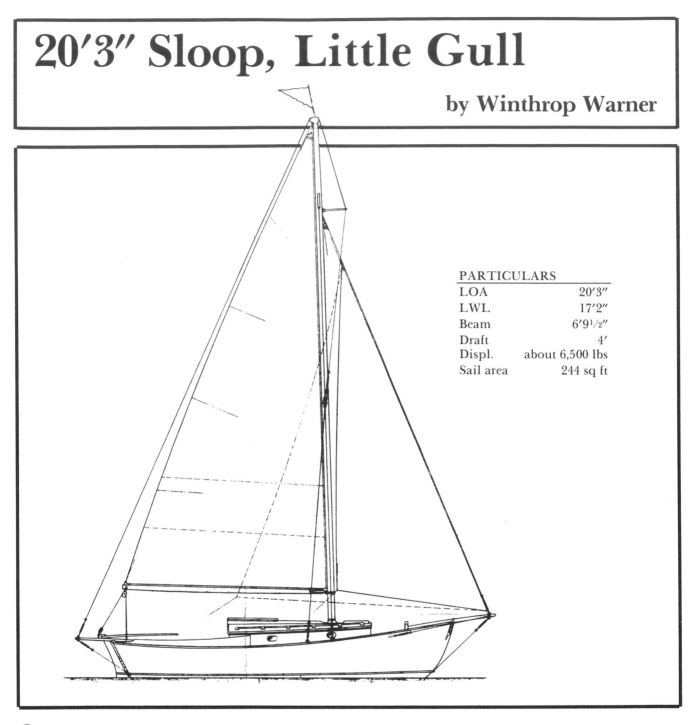

PARTICULARS

LOA	20'3"
LWL	17'2"
Beam	6'9½"
Draft	4'
Displ.	about 6,500 lbs
Sail area	244 sq ft

So well proportioned is this salty little cruiser that she looks like a boat half again longer than her 20'3" hull length. And so wholesome is her design that she should be able to face up to about any sea or wind one is apt to find; with competent handling, she'd even do well in offshore sailing. An outside ballast keel of cast lead makes her self-righting, and a small-volume self-bailing cockpit keeps her from taking on much water in the unlikely event of a knockdown.

She's as handy to use as she is safe. Her rig has but two sails; the mainsail, like most, needs no sheet-tending when tacking, and her working jib, although shown loose-footed with two separate sheets, can be (and has been on at least one boat built to this design) fitted with a boom of its own which will allow it to tack like the mainsail without sheet-tending. The short bowsprit is a great place from which to rig the anchor, keeping the foredeck clear and clean. And the boat

has been designed for an inboard engine—a real convenience, but a feature rarely found on so small a craft.

You must realize that Little Gull is only 20' long, and because of her small size, cruising accommodations are limited. She has sitting headroom, two berths, and a basic galley. There's a boxed-in toilet shown as well. Its's a perfectly comfortable arrangement if your expectations aren't too great, and one which could be altered to suit individual needs without affecting how the boat looks or how she sails.

Little Gull is a little boat with the character and characteristics of one nearly twice her size. She's a boat that you'll always enjoy approaching as she rides to her mooring. And in any harbor she'll draw admirers.

The plans are in 11 sheets—including sail plan, lines, offsets, construction, cabin plan, spar plan, boom detail, running rigging, and tang details. WB Plan No. 54. $150.00.

Plan 54

DESCRIPTION
Hull type: Round-bottomed, outside-ballasted keel
    boat
Rig: Sloop
Construction: Carvel planked over steamed frames
Headroom/cabin (between beams):   About 4'7"

PERFORMANCE
*Suitable for: Open ocean
*Intended capacity: 3-4 daysailing, 2 cruising

*See page 112 for further information.

Trailerable: With difficulty
Propulsion: Sail w/auxiliary
Speed (knots):   3-5

BUILDING DATA:
Skill needed: Advanced
Lofting required: Yes
*Alternative construction: Cold-molded, strip

PLANS DATA
No. of sheets: 11
Level of detail: Above average
Cost per set: $150.00
WB Plan No. 54

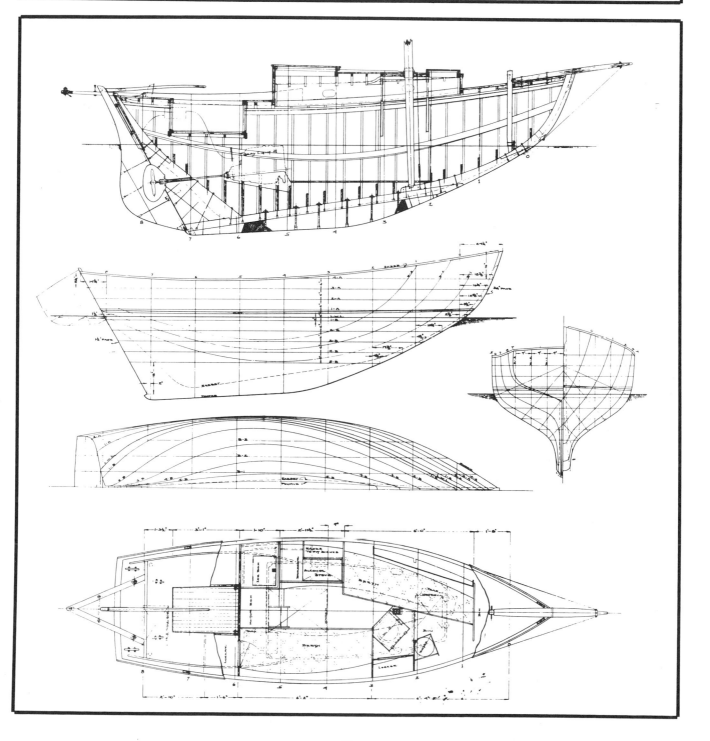

21'1" Gaff Sloop

by Nelson Zimmer

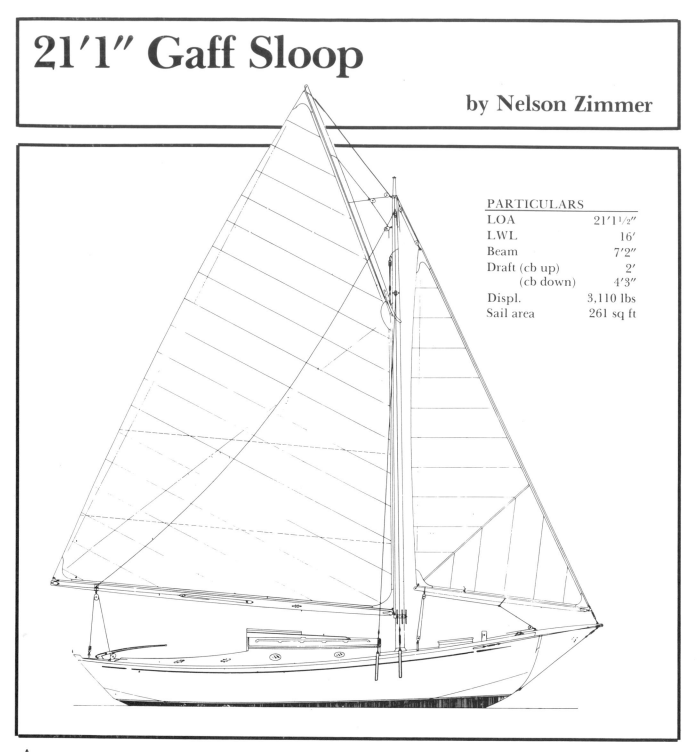

PARTICULARS

LOA	21'1½"
LWL	16'
Beam	7'2"
Draft (cb up)	2'
(cb down)	4'3"
Displ.	3,110 lbs
Sail area	261 sq ft

According to Mr. Zimmer, this little centerboard sloop, designed in 1946, has drawn inquiries throughout the years—an indication of her wide appeal.

Though only 21' overall, the V-bottomed sloop has many of the features of a real deepwater vessel—a strong sheer, a bold stem profile, a well-proportioned cabin trunk, and a high-peaked gaff sail plan. The hull is beamy, with a very short aft overhang ending in a counter stern. Handling her would be very easy. Both her mainsail and jib are self-tending, and there are no running backstays to worry about. She should be reasonably fast and quite stable, with a sturdy oak backbone and 750 pounds of inside ballast. The boat displaces 3,100 pounds.

The five sheets of plans are very carefully detailed, and construction is straightforward and well thought out. She has sawn frames at each station, around which the hull is set up and planked. Intermediate frames reinforce the bottom planking, while the topside seams are backed up with full-length fore-and-aft battens. Her hull is strengthened by a full set of lodging and hanging knees—unusual to see in so small a boat.

Below, simplicity is the theme. There are two settee berths, a single built-in locker, and a large platform forward for gear stowage, to which a large hatch in the foredeck gives easy access. An outboard engine is optional.

This strong, sprightly little sloop is best suited to day-sailing and camping/cruising.

Included in the plans are a special "Spar and Fitting Details" sheet (see WB No. 58) and a complete rigging and block list of 60 items. WB Plan No. 44. $75.00.

Plan 44

DESCRIPTION

Hull type: V-bottomed, centerboard

Rig: Gaff sloop

Construction: Carvel planking over sawn frames

Headroom/cabin (between beams):   About 3'7"

Featured in Design Section: WB No. 58

PERFORMANCE

*Suitable for: Somewhat protected waters

*Intended capacity: 2-4 daysailing, 2 cruising

See page 112 for further information.

Trailerable: Yes

Propulsion: Sail

Speed (knots):   3-5

BUILDING DATA

Skill needed: Intermediate to advanced

Lofting required: Yes

*Alternative construction: Strip

PLANS DATA

No. of sheets: 5

Level of detail: Above average

Cost per set: $75.00

WB Plan No. 44

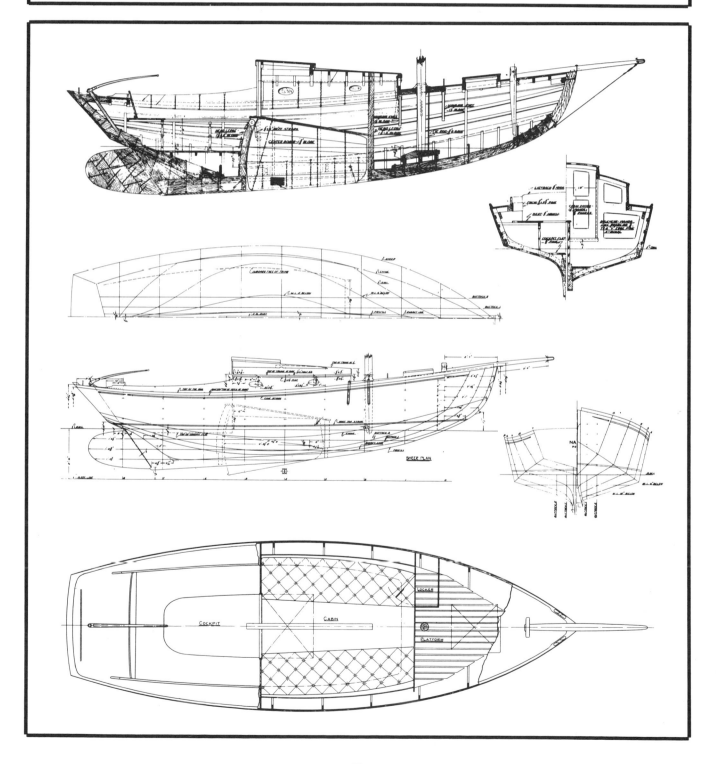

21'2" Double-Ended Sloop

by John G. Alden

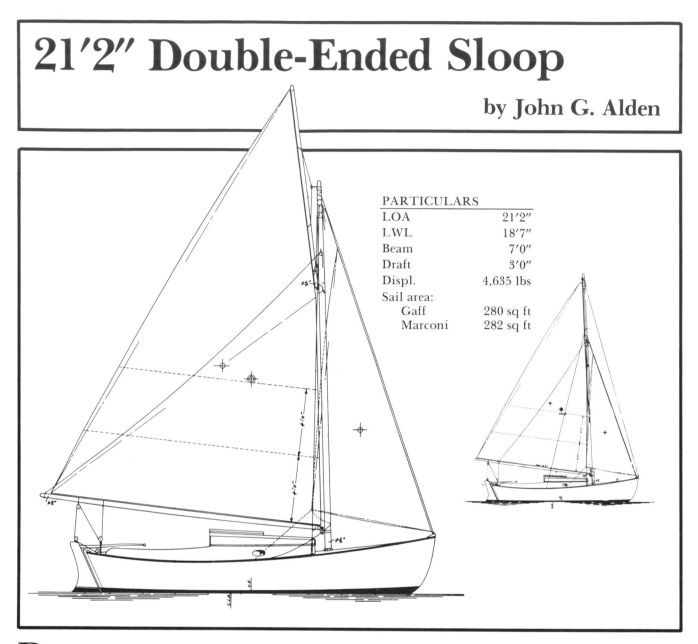

PARTICULARS	
LOA	21'2"
LWL	18'7"
Beam	7'0"
Draft	3'0"
Displ.	4,635 lbs
Sail area:	
Gaff	280 sq ft
Marconi	282 sq ft

Double-enders have long been held in high esteem as seakeepers, from Viking longships to pinky schooners and North Sea Pilot cutters. It shouldn't be surprising, then, to see this remarkably small variation on a theme. There is considerably more boat here than meets the eye, for, like the 24' Fenwick Williams yawl, this boat would not only be fast and weatherly, but also remarkably spacious below.

Five of these 21-footers were built in 1929, after which time the Depression must have caused many to forget about such things. But we can't bear to see the design forgotten, for here could be a wonderfully versatile cruising boat.

Two rigs are offered—a high-peaked gaff and a marconi—and both provide practically equal amounts of sail area. The taller mast of the marconi rig, of course, requires more stays (eight as opposed to three), but it also requires one less spar (the gaff) and one less halyard. Like the gunter rig, the nearly vertical gaff presents a complication in the reefing, since the peak halyard must be seized or clipped all the way out on the gaff in order for the sail to set properly with reefs tucked in. On the other hand, the running backstay arrangement in the marconi rig presents its own complications (which will surely occur with more frequency), so

we tend to favor the gaff.

Whatever the rig, this is a wonderfully simple boat. Her construction is rugged and straightforward, yet she is a finely modeled hull (see those hollow waterlines and that finely chiseled forefoot). Tiller steering, outboard rudder, a very simple cockpit arrangement, and spliced eyes rather than tangs for the standing rigging contribute to the simplicity.

Her layout below is simple but comfortable, with two berths, a stove, ice chest, dish locker, hanging locker, and stowage beneath platforms. Indeed, she is very charming and cozy. Having been designed in 1928, the engine access hatch and bridge deck configuration were designed for a contemporary auxiliary. A modern auxiliary might require some alteration to the plan. The engine compartment is separated from the cabin by means of a watertight bulkhead.

The plans are only moderately detailed, and some boatbuilding experience is required to produce a result that is worthy of the design. But it's well worth the effort, for this is a fine little boat. Plans consist of lines, offsets, sail plans (marconi and gaff), cabin plan, construction plan, two ballast-keel plans (lead and iron), specifications list, and a marconi rig block list. WB Plan No. 1. $135.00.

Plan 1

DESCRIPTION

Hull type: Round-bottomed double-ender
Rig: Gaff or marconi sloop
Construction: Carvel planked over steamed frames
Headroom/cabin (between beams):   about 4'2"
Featured in Design Section: WB No. 40

PERFORMANCE

*Suitable for: Open ocean
*Intended capacity: 2-4 daysailing, 2 cruising

* See page 112 for further information.

Trailerable: With difficulty
Propulsion: Sail w/auxiliary
Speed (knots):   3-5

BUILDING DATA:

Skill needed: Advanced
Lofting required: Yes
*Alternative construction: Cold-molded, strip

PLANS DATA

No. of sheets: 7
Level of detail: Average
Cost per set: $135.00
WB Plan No. 1

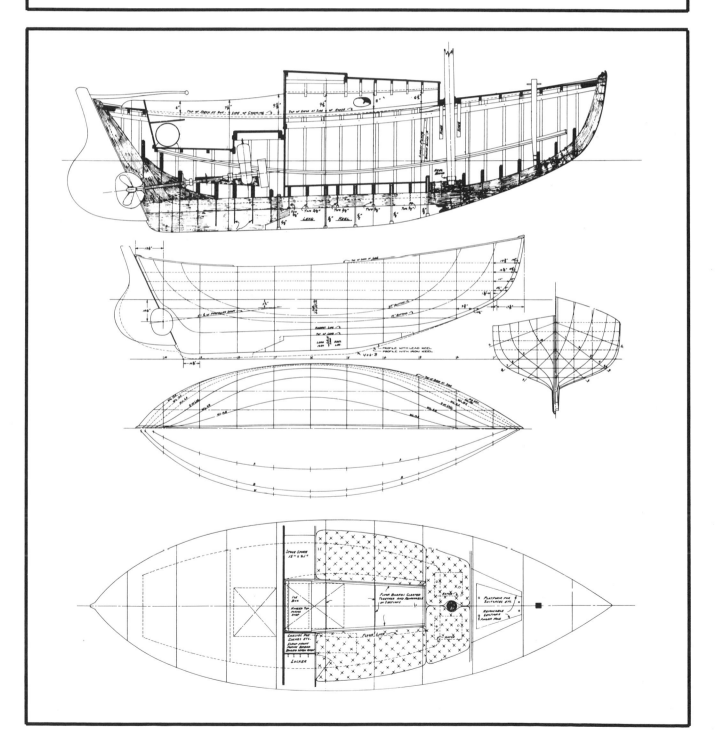

22'11" Yawl Blue Moon

by Thomas Gillmer

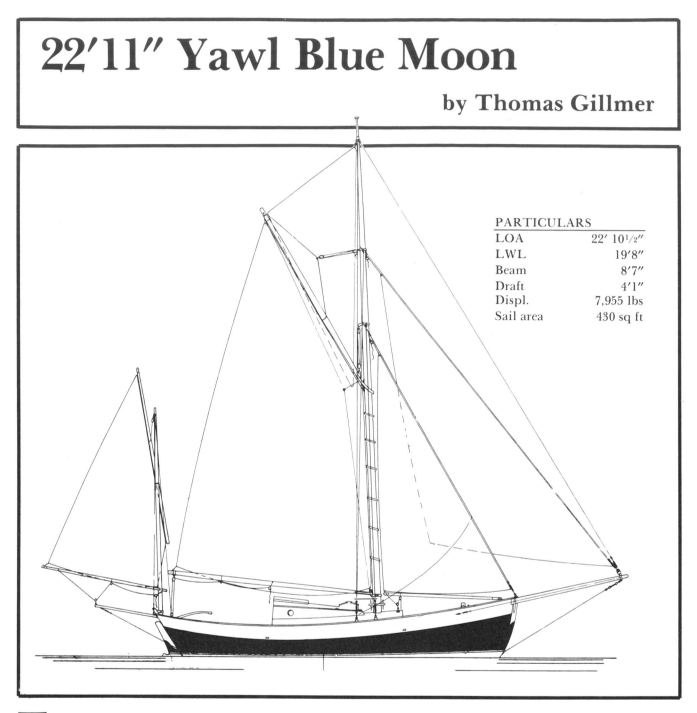

PARTICULARS	
LOA	22' 10½"
LWL	19'8"
Beam	8'7"
Draft	4'1"
Displ.	7,955 lbs
Sail area	430 sq ft

The designer's aim of maximum cruising ability, seaworthiness, utility, and comfort in a craft of minimum dimensions was admirably achieved in this salty 23-footer inspired by the traditional oyster boats that once worked along the southern coast of England near Falmouth. These so-called Falmouth Quay Punts were all-weather boats, able to make distance to windward even when under shortened sail in a blow.

For strength and for room below, she has been designed with a flush deck amidships rather than the usual big trunk cabin and, although there isn't standing headroom under this deck, you can come closer to an erect posture under the raised companionway hatch.

The gaff-yawl rig with its topsail and two headsails may not be the easiest to handle, but it does allow many convenient variations in shortening sail when the wind comes up, and it gives the skipper endless opportunity to experiment with sail trim. For any youngsters aboard, Blue Moon has plenty of strings to pull; in fact she's a real little ship.

Although her designer didn't develop Blue Moon for construction by amateurs and drew her plans with only an average amount of detail, he does pass on the thought that there is nothing complicated about the way she's put together—just a straightforward job of old-fashioned boatbuilding.

Boats have been built to this design since 1946, and they've been cruised far and wide, one boat making a 900-mile ocean passage from the Azores to Portugal. Her designer says of her, "She behaves like a well-trained animal, waiting attentively as the mooring is let go. She is subordinate, yet responsive. She always gave me a feeling of relaxed security as the water surged off under her quarter."

The plans are in nine sheets, including sail plan, lines, offsets, structural plan, lead ballast profile, watertight cockpit detail, cabin profile, accommodation and spar plans. WB No. 59. $150.00.

Plan 59

DESCRIPTION
Hull type: Round-bottomed, outside-ballasted keel boat
Rig: Gaff yawl
Construction: Carvel planking over steamed frames
Headroom/cabin (between beams):   About 4'9"
Featured in Design Section: WB No. 2
PERFORMANCE
*Suitable for: Open ocean

*Intended capacity: 3-6 daysailing, 2 cruising
Trailerable: With difficulty; permit required
Propulsion: Sail w/auxiliary
Speed (knots):   3-6
BUILDING DATA:
Skill needed: Advanced
Lofting required: Yes
*Alternative construction: Cold-molded, strip
PLANS DATA
No. of sheets: 9
Level of detail: Average
Cost per set: $150.00
WB Plan No. 59

* See page 112 for further information.

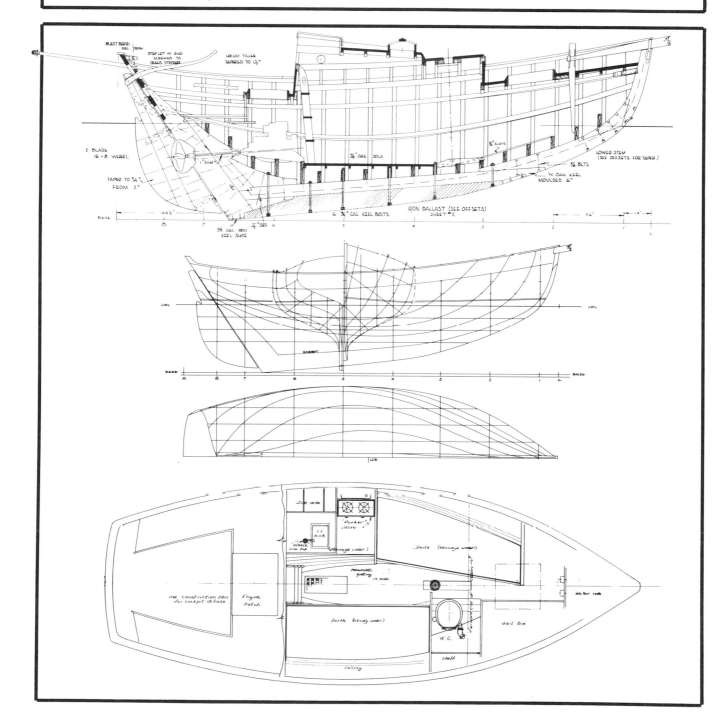

24' Gaff Yawl

by Fenwick C. Williams

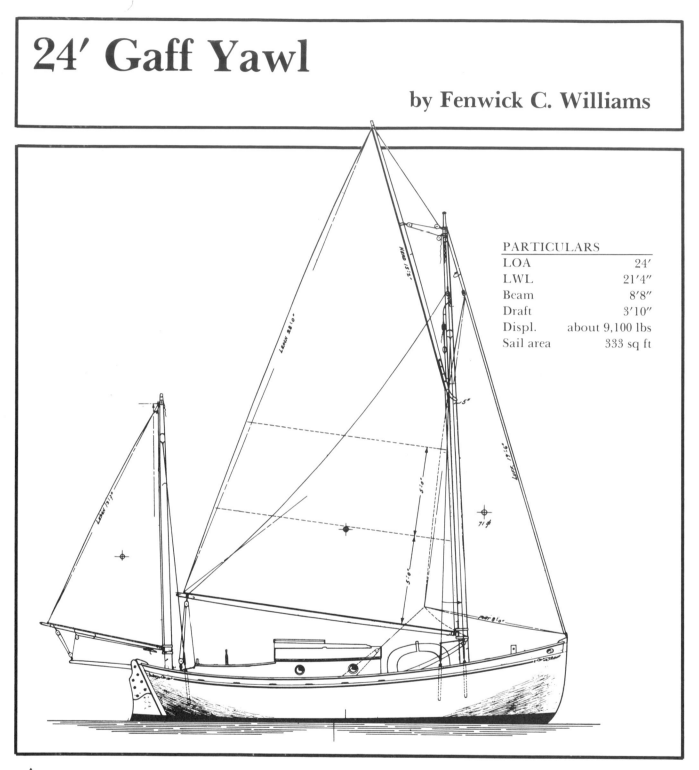

PARTICULARS	
LOA	24'
LWL	21'4"
Beam	8'8"
Draft	3'10"
Displ.	about 9,100 lbs
Sail area	333 sq ft

Although designer Fenwick C. Williams is best known for his exquisite cruising catboats, his 24' Gaff Yawl has proven herself to be an unusually fine combination of all the factors making up a good boat. With outside ballast, short, balanced ends, and generous freeboard, she is very seaworthy. Her rig is simple, making her easily handled. She's roomy below and has lots of deck space. And she's certainly sweet to look at. (See "ANNIE," WB No. 41.)

Designed in 1933, only two of the yawls were built then, and both ended up on the Great Lakes. It's not surprising, though, that interest in this particular design should resurface. Her good lines, comfort, stability, and swift and responsive nature have no doubt influenced the building of two more of them recently, one in Maine, and the other on

Long Island.

The one we know the most about was ANNIE, built by Arundel Shipyard in Kennebunkport. She was planked with cedar over oak, fastened with bronze, her ballast keel was lead, and the decks were teak. Her auxiliary power was a Sabb 8-hp diesel, and her cost was in the $40,000-$50,000 range. With an overall length of 24', an 8'8" beam, and a draft of 3'10", she accommodates two or four persons.

Considerable boatbuilding skill is needed, however, along with quite a commitment of time and money. We think she'd be well worth it. The seven-sheet set of plans includes lines and offsets, sail plans, construction plan, cabin plan, engine installation/cockpit layout, and an alternative lead keel plan. WB Plan No. 16. $125.00.

Plan 16

DESCRIPTION

Hull type: Round-bottomed double-ender
with outside ballast keel

Rig: Yawl w/gaff main & marconi mizzen

Construction: Carvel planked over steamed frames

Headroom/cabin (between beams):   about 5'6"

Featured in Design Section: WB No. 28

PERFORMANCE

*Suitable for: Open ocean

*Intended capacity: 4-6 daysailing, 2 cruising

Trailerable: With difficulty; permit required

Propulsion: Sail and auxiliary inboard engine

Speed (knots):   3-6

BUILDING DATA

Skill needed: Advanced

Lofting required: Yes

*Alternative construction: Strip or cold-molded

Helpful WB issues: WB No. 41

PLANS DATA

No. of sheets: 7

Level of detail: Average

Cost per set: $125.00

WB Plan No. 16

See page 112 for further information.

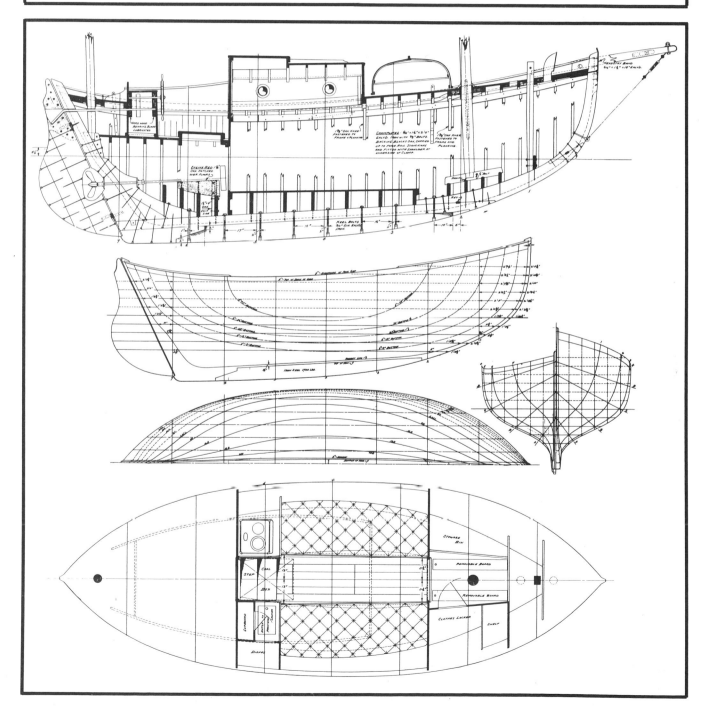

—73—

24'11" Keel/Centerboard Sloop

by John G. Alden

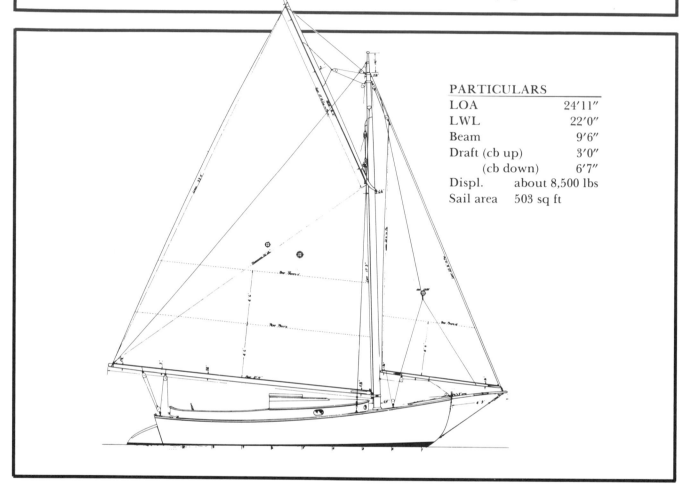

PARTICULARS

LOA	24'11"
LWL	22'0"
Beam	9'6"
Draft (cb up)	3'0"
(cb down)	6'7"
Displ.	about 8,500 lbs
Sail area	503 sq ft

Although the records indicate that no boats were built to this 1929 design, we are quite fascinated by its potential as a fast and able cruiser. We're also impressed with the rather elaborate construction details, which are well worth a careful study.

It's very easy to speculate on the influences that have governed the design of different boats, but the roots of this one are most assuredly the Cape Cod catboat. The differences are less beam, a stretched-out forebody, and of course the gaff sloop rig. The rig is quite simple, in spite of its power, with only three stays supporting the mast and with the forestay tension coming from the bobstay and shroud turnbuckles. The self-tending jib is rigged with lazyjacks, and the main would be somewhat easier to handle while lowering if it were similarly rigged.

This sloop has a number of distinctive details about her, beginning with the beautiful steam-bent house sides and coamings (the latter being bent around vertical staving). She has wheel-steering, but an alternate tiller-steering arrangement is provided for. The after end of the bowsprit is fashioned and pinned to form a mooring cleat so that neither a conventional cleat nor a mooring bit is required.

There are several interesting details in her construction, including the slotted cast-iron keel (1,500 pounds), the numerous lodging knees, the mast-step/partners tie-rod,

the strong centerboard case, and the built-up rudder.

Accommodations are very simple, with two berths in the main cabin, and a single berth and head in the forward cabin. The galley stove is located just aft of the forward bulkhead, and the drop-leaf table on the centerboard case is the working surface. Interestingly, the forward third of the case is cut down to the level of the cabin sole, which provides considerably more freedom of movement in that area. The bridge deck at the aft end of the cabin provides the additional room needed below as well as increased transverse strength (always desirable in a sailing hull). Beneath the bridge deck are a stowage box and an icebox, both of which are removable for cleaning or painting. A 25-gallon water tank supplies the boat through a simple gravity-feed line.

A watertight bulkhead separates the cabin from the engine compartment, and access to the engine is through a hatch in the cockpit sole (designed to accommodate the engine selected).

We noted provisions for running backstays with a marconi rig configuration, but it is assumed that the rig was never developed. (We'd probably recommend the gaff, anyway.)

This is quite a fine little boat, we think. Plans include sail plan, lines, offsets, construction, iron keel plan, cabin plan, and a specifications list. Price for the set is $135.

Plan 2

DESCRIPTION

Hull type: Round-bottomed, outside-ballasted
 keel/cb boat

Rig: Gaff sloop

Construction: Carvel planked over steamed frames

Headroom/cabin (between beams): About 4'7"

Featured in Design Section: WB No. 40

PERFORMANCE

*Suitable for: Open ocean

*Intended capacity: 3-6 daysailing, 2 cruising

See page 112 for further information.

Trailerable: With difficulty; permit required

Propulsion: Sail w/auxiliary

Speed (knots):   3-6

BUILDING DATA

Skill needed: Advanced

Lofting required: Yes

*Alternative construction: Cold-molded, strip

PLANS DATA

No. of sheets: 5

Level of detail: Average

Cost per set: $135.00

WB Plan No. 2

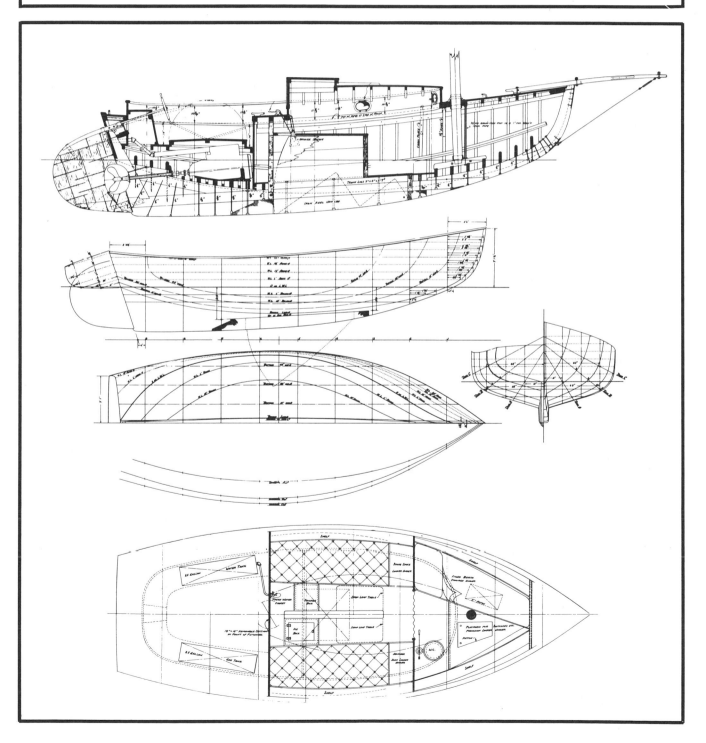

25' Pemaquid Type Friendship Sloop

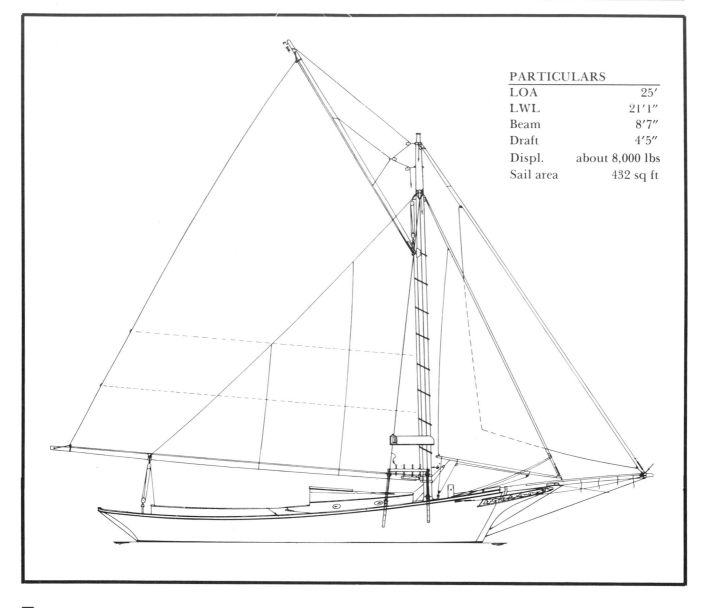

PARTICULARS	
LOA	25'
LWL	21'1"
Beam	8'7"
Draft	4'5"
Displ.	about 8,000 lbs
Sail area	432 sq ft

It would be hard to find a more seaworthy, dependable, and beautiful traditional boat than the Friendship sloop in the hierarchy of great designs. Originally developed as fishing boats, they were surprisingly fast on a reach (they had to beat their competitors to market with their catch), steady and dry running off the wind even in a messy sea, were easy to steer, and sat quietly at anchor. In the hands of a sailor who understood her, the Friendship sloop could heave to at sea with ease, and in a blow brought him home safe and enthusiastic about his vessel.

The first PEMAQUID, a fine example of her type, was built in 1914 by Abdon Carter in Bremen, Maine, and her lines were taken off in 1935 by the late Charles MacGregor. The modified version of the Pemaquid is drawn with the builder and yachtsman in mind. She is a lovely boat with a sweeping sheer, the graceful, traditional arc in her

bowsprit, and a curved schooner transom. Pemaquid's dimensions are 25' LOA, 21'1" LWL, 8'7" beam, and 4'5" draft. Her gaff mainsail is 313 sq ft, and she carries a jib and staysail, which gives her a total sail area of 432 sq ft. The original Pemaquid had all inside ballast, but this redrawn version substitutes 2,000 pounds of outside lead ballast while retaining 300 pounds inside. She is snug below with a larger cabin than the original, including two berths and a small galley.

The four sheets of well-detailed plans were drawn by Jay Hanna from information supplied by Bald Mountain Boat Works, Geerd N. Hendel, N.A., Malcolm H. Brewer, Master Boatbuilder, Henry F. Bohndell, Sailmaker, and the original Pemaquid drawings by H.I. Chapelle. Included in the plans are lines (with developed transom), offsets, sail plan, and construction plan. WB Plan No. 46. $60.00.

Plan 46

DESCRIPTION

Hull type: Round-bottomed, outside-ballasted keel boat

Rig: Gaff sloop

Construction: Carvel planking over steamed frames

Headroom/cabin (between beams):   About 4'4"

PERFORMANCE

*Suitable for: Open ocean

*Intended capacity: 3-6 daysailing, 2 cruising

See page 112 for further information.

Trailerable: With difficulty; permit required

Propulsion: Sail w/auxiliary

Speed (knots):   3-6

BUILDING DATA

Skill needed: Advanced

Lofting required: Yes

*Alternative construction: Strip

PLANS DATA

No. of sheets: 4

Level of detail: Average

Cost per set: $60.00

WB Plan No. 46

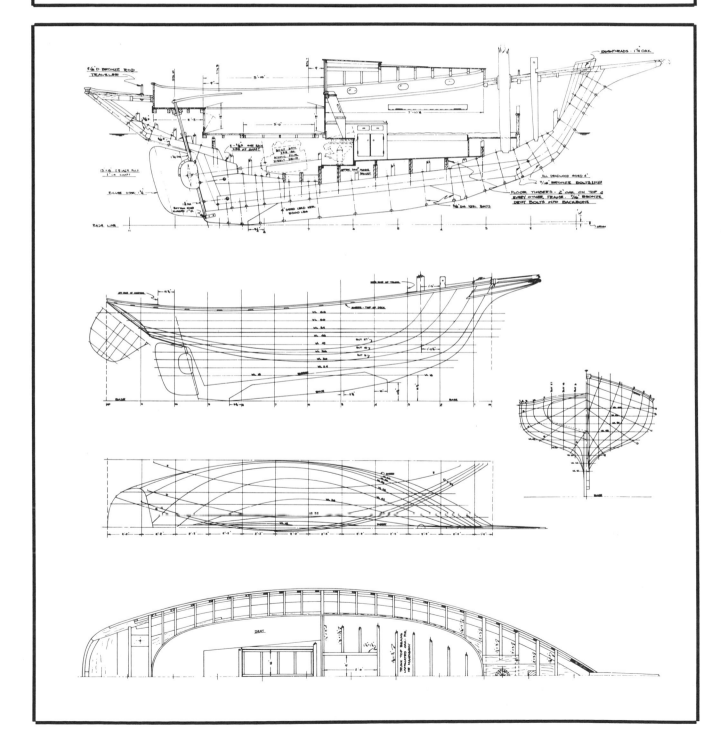

25'7" Sea Bird Yawl

by T.F. Day and C.D. Mower

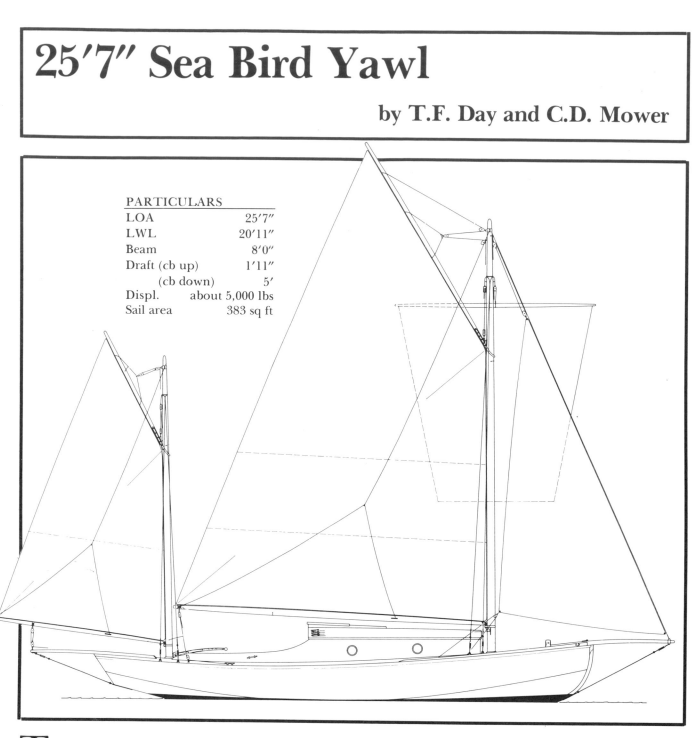

PARTICULARS

LOA	25'7"
LWL	20'11"
Beam	8'0"
Draft (cb up)	1'11"
(cb down)	5'
Displ.	about 5,000 lbs
Sail area	383 sq ft

The V-bottomed yawl Sea Bird has occupied a legendary place in the annals of yachting since the first news of her launching in 1901. Conceived by Tom Day, founding editor of *The Rudder*, and drawn up by Charles Mower, with construction details by Larry Huntington, she was a successful blend of considerable experience. Her simple form and straightforward construction made her an appealing boat to those of modest means, especially in light of her reputation for being handy and able.

As a centerboard craft she left little to be desired in performance, but her accommodations were severely limited by the presence of the centerboard trunk in the cabin. As she was built for extended cruising, and as Tom Day desired a happy and comfortable crew for his little yawl, she was converted to a keel craft in the spring of 1902. Though he was not as happy with her motion at sea, Capt. Day acknowledged that she was on the whole more comfortable,

and no less able. Indeed, so convinced was he of her abilities that in the summer of 1911 he sailed her across the Atlantic with a crew of two.

It isn't well known just how many boats were built to these plans, although they were built all over the world. And many revised versions were designed and built as well.

Our objective in having the plans redrawn was to ensure the preservation of the lines and details of this very important craft, both for now and for the future. For its intended purpose it is certainly a timeless design, and might be well worth considering for those who desire a simple and inexpensive cruising boat with the potential to make long passages.

Plans are drawn at a scale of one inch to the foot and include lines, offsets, sail plan, construction plan, cabin plan, deck plan, details, and keel conversion. Price for the complete set (seven sheets) is $75. WB Plan No. 3.

Plan 3

DESCRIPTION
Hull type: V-bottomed
Rig: Gaff yawl
Construction: Carvel planked over sawn frames
Headroom/cabin (between beams): about 4'2"

PERFORMANCE
*Suitable for: Somewhat protected waters
*Intended capacity: 2-4 daysailing, 2 cruising
Trailerable: Yes, permit required

See page 112 for further information.

Propulsion: Sail
Speed (knots): 3-6

BUILDING DATA:
Skill needed: Intermediate to advanced
Lofting required: Yes
Alternative construction: Strip
*Helpful WB issues: WB Nos. 43 & 44

PLANS DATA
No. of sheets: 7
Level of detail: Above average
Cost per set: $75.00
WB Plan No. 3

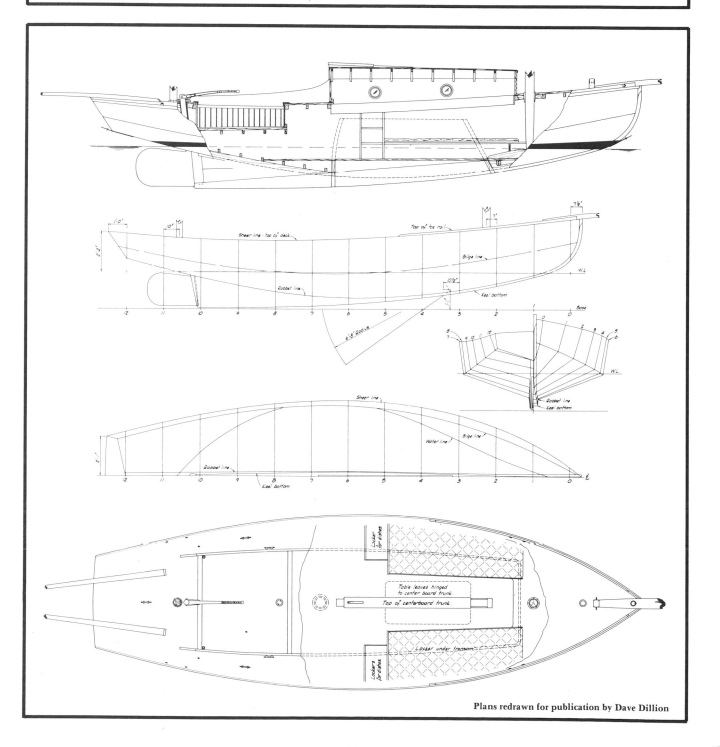

Plans redrawn for publication by Dave Dillion

25'7" Plywood Sea Bird Yawl

by Charles G. MacGregor

PARTICULARS

LOA	25'7"
LWL	20'3"
Beam	8'1"
Draft (cb up)	2'6"
(cb down)	4'0"
Displ.	4,313 lbs
Sail area	379 sq ft

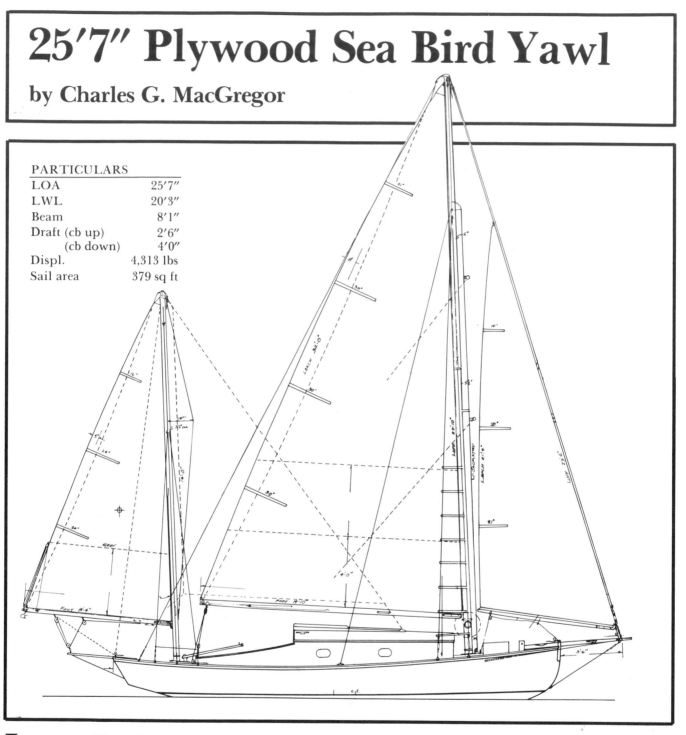

In response to *WoodenBoat*'s articles on Thomas Fleming Day and the original V-bottomed Sea Bird (WB Nos. 43 and 44), a reader announced that he had a set of blueprints for Charles MacGregor's plywood version. WoodenBoat had been trying to locate these drawings, and promptly purchased them. We were delighted to find them crisp and detailed, the basis for an education in proper plywood construction.

MacGregor, a pioneer in plywood boat design, was among the first to see plywood's potential for light, strong construction. The lines of this version, published in WB No. 50, are identical to those of the original Sea Bird, except for the increased draft. But the accommodations within the cabin are considerably more spacious, due to the changed shape of the centerboard—though the boat as shown still accommodates only two, cozily. It is claimed, however, that

the smaller footwell (instead of a cockpit used in the original) allows for installation of two quarter-berths, although the extra berths are not indicated in the drawings.

The most striking differences would be in improved performance. The several hundred pounds saved in hull weight have been transferred to the lead ballast keel, thus increasing stability. The rig has been changed from gaff to a more efficient marconi, and three squaresails and a mizzen staysail have been added. A light outboard installation is shown for auxiliary power.

The plywood Sea Bird is an excellent example of a safe and comfortable cruiser that can be built for relatively little money. The plans consist of ten sheets, including: sail and rigging plan, lines and offsets, frames and bulkheads, construction, deck framing, mainmast detail, mast and yard detail, trailer plan and details. WB Plan No. 35. $75.00

Plan 35

DESCRIPTION

Hull type: V-bottomed, hard-chined, keel/cb
   boat
Rig: Marconi yawl
Construction: Plywood planking over sawn frames
Headroom/cabin (between beams):   about 4'7"
Featured in Design Section: WB No. 50

PERFORMANCE

*Suitable for: Somewhat protected waters

*Intended capacity: 2-4 daysailing, 2 cruising
Trailerable: Yes, plans for trailer included
Propulsion: Sail w/outboard auxiliary
Speed (knots):   3-6

BUILDING DATA

Skill needed: Intermediate
Lofting required: Yes
*Alternative construction: None

PLANS DATA

No. of sheets: 9
Level of detail: Average
Cost per set: $75.00
WB Plan No. 35

See page 112 for further information.

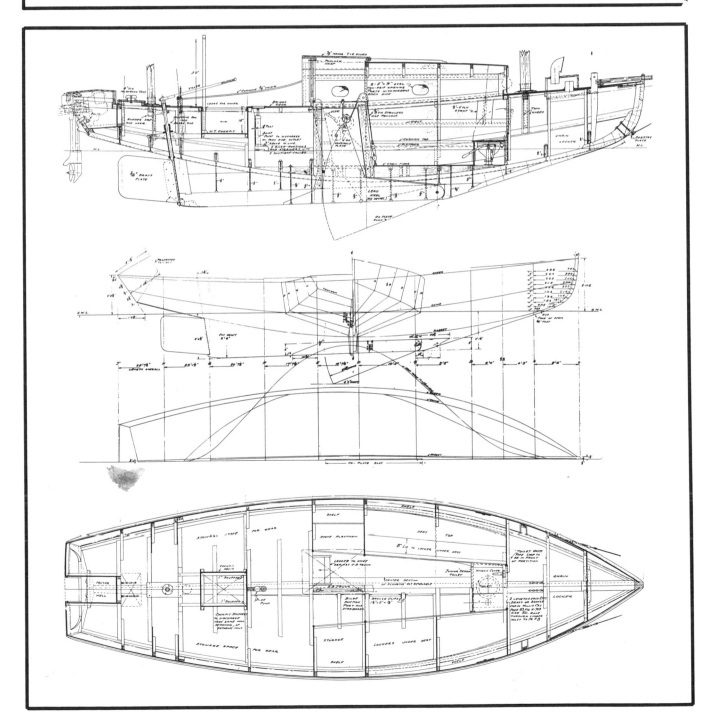

26' Gaff Sloop

by Wilder B. Harris

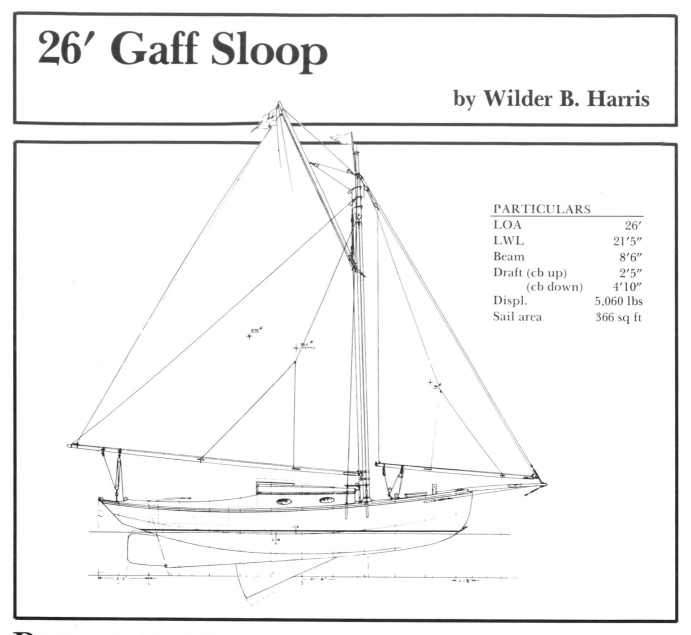

PARTICULARS	
LOA	26'
LWL	21'5"
Beam	8'6"
Draft (cb up)	2'5"
(cb down)	4'10"
Displ.	5,060 lbs
Sail area	366 sq ft

Bill Harris, who designed this lovely little pocket cruiser about 25 years ago, has had a wide-ranging career in yacht and vessel design which started when he joined the John G. Alden office in the 1920s. As "house" designer for a number of New England boatyards and offices, his name isn't well known, but his wonderful eye and hand have given beauty and grace to many a boat—the Concordia 28, 31, and 33 (whose plans are sold by Wooden-Boat and are described elsewhere in this catalog) among them. This 26-footer, however, came out under his own name and was designed for sailing in the shallow waters of the Gulf Coast.

Her hull is reminiscent of the Sea Bird yawl also included in these pages. Giving her a similar salty sheer, low freeboard, and rising chine, Bill Harris has, if anything, come up with a more handsome boat; he certainly has provided a grand opportunity to select an attractive alternative to Sea Bird's rig. With no mizzen, but with the same type of stout mainmast that will stand without help from running backstays or elaborate standing rigging, with both a mainsail and jib that self-tend when tacking, and rigged with the lazyjacks and multi-part sheeting arrangement shown, handling this boat under sail will be a dream.

There's enough sail area to keep her going in light breezes, and when the wind dies altogether, you'll find she glides along fine under oar—either by sculling or rowing. An outboard motor hung over the stern or in a well could, of course, be added.

Finding storage space for gear and provisions aboard this boat is no problem—as she's laid out, there's room under the afterdeck reachable from the cockpit, more space in the bins behind the settees in the cabin, and under the foredeck is the biggest area of all for stowage. Accommodations, even for two people, are limited, however, and you should realize this before getting too committed. The cabin is small in area as well as in height because the designer's reigning priority was to come up with a boat that looked right to the sailor's eye. With this goal in mind, there's little doubt that the boat was a great success.

Like all sawn-frame V-bottomed boats, this one would be suitable for amateur construction. And for basic cruising, even when sailing in pretty nasty weather, she'd be finest-kind.

Plans include four sheets: Sail plan, lines, offsets, and construction.
WB Plan No. 62. $75.00.

Plan 62

DESCRIPTION
Hull type: V-bottomed centerboard boat
Rig: Gaff sloop
Construction: Carvel planked over sawn frames
Headroom/cabin (between beams): About 4'

PERFORMANCE
*Suitable for: Somewhat protected waters
*Intended capacity: 2-4 daysailing, 2 cruising

See page 112 for further information.

Trailerable: With difficulty, permit required
Propulsion: Sail
Speed (knots):   3-6

BUILDING DATA:
Skill needed: Intermediate to advanced
Lofting required: Yes
*Alternative construction: Strip. plywood

PLANS DATA
No. of sheets: 5
Level of detail: Average
Cost per set: $75.00
WB Plan No. 62

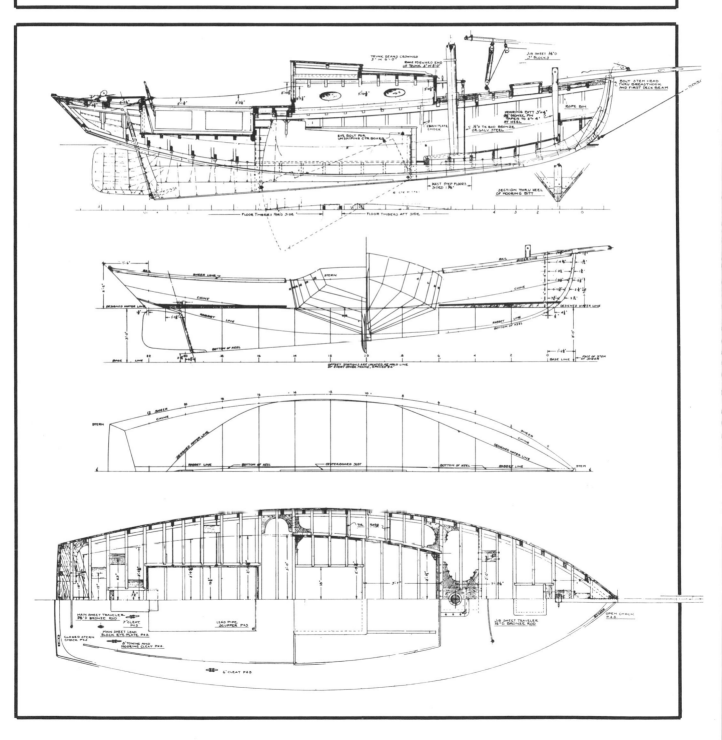

26' Pilot Sloop/Schooner

by George Stadel

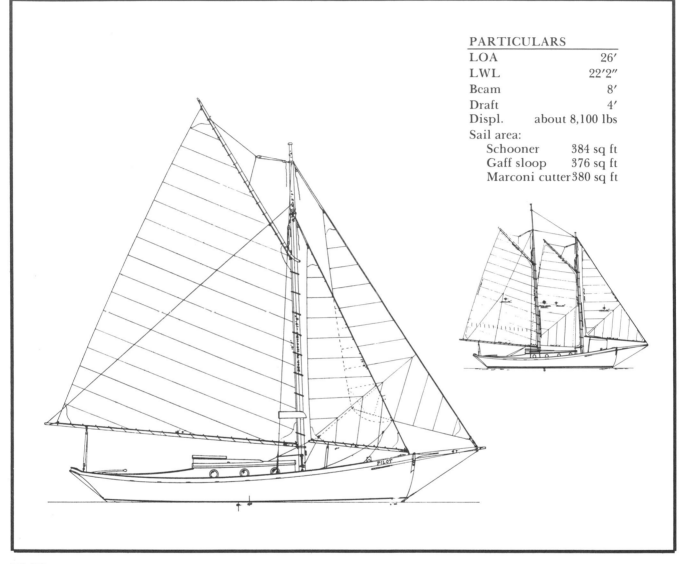

PARTICULARS

LOA	26'
LWL	22'2"
Beam	8'
Draft	4'
Displ.	about 8,100 lbs
Sail area:	
Schooner	384 sq ft
Gaff sloop	376 sq ft
Marconi cutter	380 sq ft

How this first of George Stadel's lovely Pilot series of designs came into being is best told by the designer himself:

"One cold winter evening before World War II, Howard Chapelle and I were kicking around ideas that would make a good cruising boat. We finally came to the conclusion that two of the best types, for use in this area at least, were the sailing fishermen and the pilot boats. The fishing schooner's freeboard would be too low and there'd be too little room below, however, if she were scaled down into a cruiser. The pilot boats, on the other hand, were relatively small to begin with. They were able and fast sailers, comfortable and quite roomy. These were all the qualities needed for a good cruiser.

"From this discussion, I drew up the first 26' Pilot. She was very successful and about 40 of them have been built over the years. Later, I went on to design others of the same shape, but in a variety of lengths from 20' to 41'."

Unquestionably, the pilot boat shape as interpreted by Stadel is beautiful from any angle, afloat or ashore. She'll sail about as well as she looks, stay at sea in comfort when other boats are hard pressed, and she'll turn heads in admiration wherever she goes. But remember, she's a small 26-footer by today's standards, with less than full headroom in her cabin. You should be willing to cruise with pretty basic accommodations, if you choose this boat as the one to build.

If you do make the Pilot your choice—and it's hard not to fall head over heels in love with her—you can rig her in a variety of ways, all of which are shown on the drawings. The original boat was a double-headsail gaff sloop; a marconi cutter and a schooner followed. All versions have the salty look of a traditional working vessel.

The plans come in 10 sheets, and include lines, offsets, construction, inboard profile and arrangement plans for sloop and schooner, and spar details, plus specifications and materials list. WB Plan No. 60. $150.00.

Plan 60

DESCRIPTION
Hull type: Round-bottomed, outside ballasted keel boat
Rig: Gaff sloop, marconi cutter or schooner
Construction: Carvel planking over steamed frames
Headroom/cabin (between beams):   About 4'8"
PERFORMANCE
*Suitable for: Open ocean
*Intended capacity: 4-6 daysailing, 4 cruising

* See page 112 for further information.

Trailerable: With difficulty
Propulsion: Sail w/auxiliary
Speed (knots):   3-6
BUILDING DATA:
Skill needed: Advanced
Lofting required: Yes
*Alternative construction: Cold-molded, strip
PLANS DATA
No. of sheets: 10
Level of detail: Average
Cost per set: $150.00
WB Plan No. 60

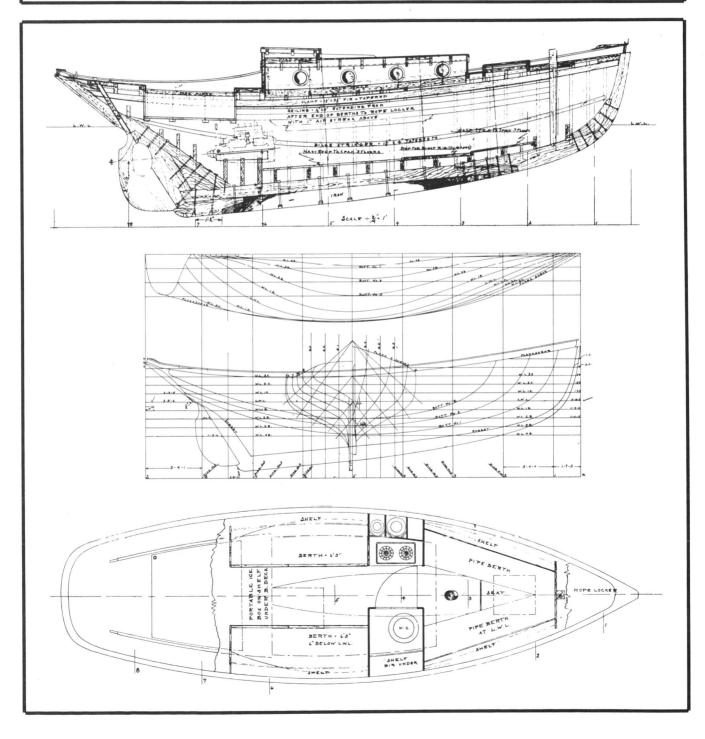

27'6" Concordia Sloop

by Concordia Company

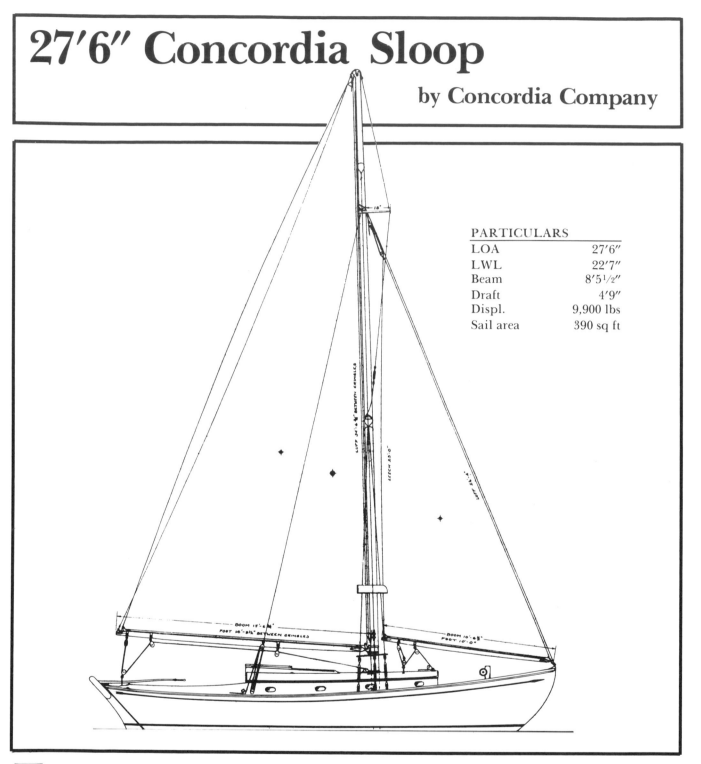

PARTICULARS	
LOA	27'6"
LWL	22'7"
Beam	8'5½"
Draft	4'9"
Displ.	9,900 lbs
Sail area	390 sq ft

The Concordia "28" was the first, and smallest, of the three short-ended cruisers created under Waldo Howland's guidance by the talented designer Wilder B. Harris in response to a need for more practical boats in the depressed mid-1930s (see WB No. 48).

In 1937, the Concordia Company was as yet a small design and brokerage office, and Howland and Harris had been working up plans for an inexpensive, practical family boat to be built, they hoped, in quantity. The "28" came into being when a customer came to Concordia seeking a big "little" three-berth cruiser that need have neither full headroom nor an auxiliary engine. The plans were drawn up, and SHAWNEE II was built in 1938.

Below deck, the cabin area of this little cruiser has plenty

of floor space, a good-sized galley with a quarter-berth opposite, two full-length fold-down "Concordia" berths ahead of that, and a fo'c's'le further forward for storage and the installation of a toilet. She has a moderate displacement, a moderate beam, a fairly hard bilge, and a wide keel, with flat transom stern and outside rudder. Her generous free-board, while in no way excessive, allows comfortable sitting headroom. Since her cabin is substantially open from end to end, she has a feeling of spaciousness and the assurance of good natural ventilation. This is a fine boat for comfortable family cruising.

The plans, which consist of seven sheets, include lines, offsets, sail plan, arrangement plan, and construction plan. WB Plan No. 32. $150.00.

Plan 32

DESCRIPTION

Hull type: Round-bottomed with outside ballast keel

Rig: Marconi sloop

Construction: Carvel planked over steamed frames

Headroom/cabin (between beams):   About 5'

Featured in Design Section: WB No. 48

PERFORMANCE

*Suitable for: Open ocean

* See page 112 for further information.

*Intended capacity: 3-8 daysailing, 3 cruising

Trailerable: With difficulty, permit required

Propulsion: Sail w/auxiliary, inboard engine

Speed (knots):   3-6

BUILDING DATA

Skill needed: Advanced

Lofting required: Yes

*Alternative construction: Cold-molded, strip

PLANS DATA

No. of sheets: 7

Level of detail: Average

Cost per set: $150.00

WB Plan No. 32

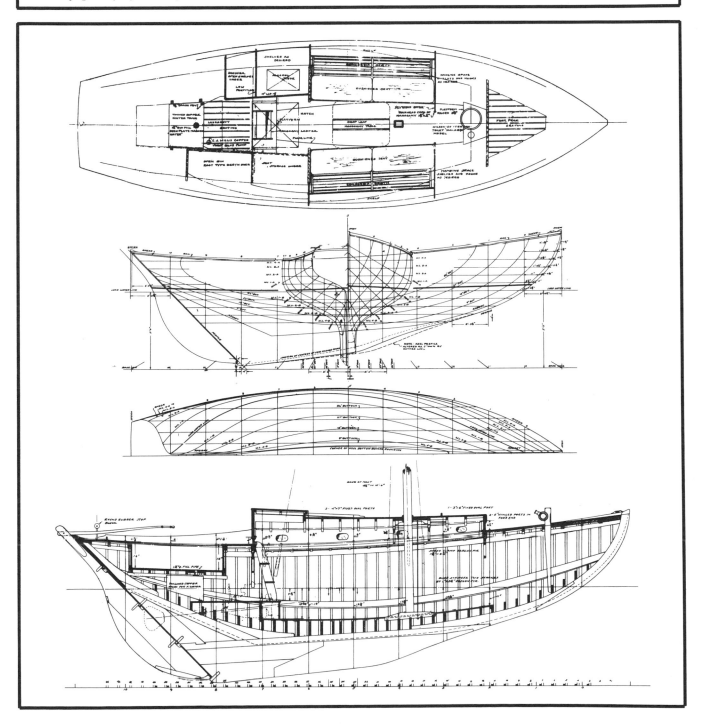

28'2" Cat-Ketch Sharpie Egret

by Commodore Ralph M. Munroe

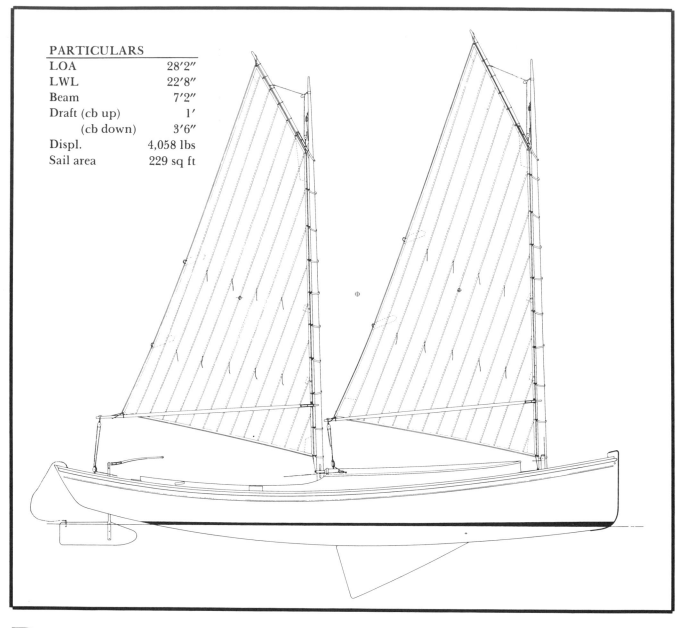

PARTICULARS

LOA	28'2"
LWL	22'8"
Beam	7'2"
Draft (cb up)	1'
(cb down)	3'6"
Displ.	4,058 lbs
Sail area	229 sq ft

Designed in 1886 as a workboat (to deliver mail), this remarkable flat-bottomed centerboard boat—Commodore Munroe's only double-ended sharpie—has no surviving original plans. But the ideas embodied in Egret as interpreted by various persons over the last 50 years have inspired a number of designs. After two years of research—comparing old photographs and records, half models, and Chapelle's take-offs—WoodenBoat has developed a set of plans that are not interpretations, but are as true to the original as possible.

Egret is Munroe's adaptation of the classic New Haven sharpie for use in Florida. She is narrower on bottom and on deck and is deeper, with a tucked-up stern and flared topsides amidships for stability. The original Egret was a legendary seakeeper, able to handle the shallows of Biscayne Bay as well as deep water, run a breaking bar, take strong winds in stride, be safely pulled up on a beach, and was fast, light, and easy to row when the occasion demanded.

As extended cruising was not her intended purpose, this boat has little in the way of accommodations—just a cuddy, with barely sitting headroom—so she is best described as what we now call a "camping-cruiser." Her rig is relatively low, and can be deeply reefed for strong breezes.

Egret is easy and inexpensive to build. The reconstructed plans, drawn by Joel White and Dave Dillion, call for straightforward hard-chine construction, and include four sheets, with lines and offsets, construction details, sail plan, sail-cutting diagram, and spar plan. WB Plan No. 42. $60.00.

Plan 12

DESCRIPTION

Hull type: Flat-bottomed, double-ended sharpie type

Rig: Cat-ketch

Construction: Single-planked sides, sawn frames, cross-planked bottom

Headroom/cabin (between beams):   About 3'4"

Featured in WB #56

PERFORMANCE

*Suitable for: Somewhat protected waters

* *See page 112 for further information.*

*Intended capacity: 2-4 daysailing, 2 cruising

Trailerable: Yes

Propulsion: Sail, oars

Speed (knots):   3-6

BUILDING DATA:

Skill needed: Intermediate

Lofting required: Yes

*Alternative construction: Plywood

PLANS DATA

No. of sheets: 4

Level of detail: Average

Cost per set: $60.00

WB Plan No. 42

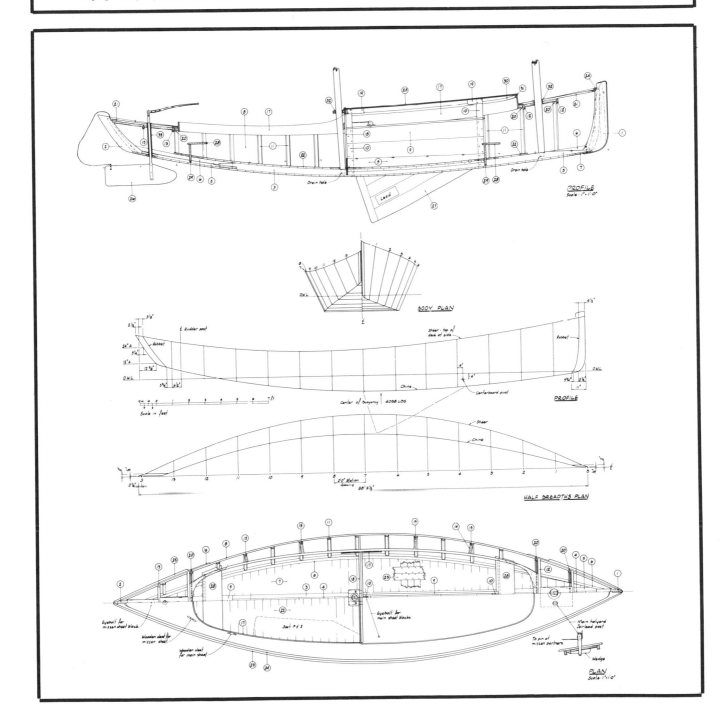

30' Sloop/Yawl Malabar Jr.

by John G. Alden

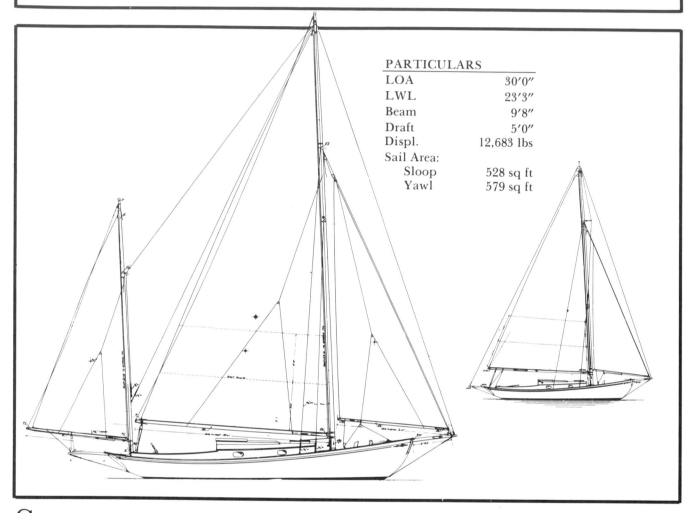

PARTICULARS	
LOA	30'0"
LWL	23'3"
Beam	9'8"
Draft	5'0"
Displ.	12,683 lbs
Sail Area:	
Sloop	528 sq ft
Yawl	579 sq ft

Several different versions of the Malabar Jr. emerged from the offices of John Alden. The first, a 29½-footer available as either a gaff or marconi sloop, came out in 1924. By that time, there was considerable interest in small, wholesome cruisers that could be cheaply built, and Alden responded to that interest. It is not well known, however, that the inspiration for this boat was the renowned and able Friendship sloop. A careful study of the Malabar Jr.'s lines will show a marked resemblance to the form of its forbears, differing primarily in the spoon bow and outside ballast/underbody profile. When studied in this light, it must be seen as quite remarkable that the accommodations to the needs of cruising were so beautifully handled.

The version published here is a combination of the second and third stages in the evolution of the type, produced during the years 1926-1928. Though there were numerous other versions as the years progressed, this example appeals to us as representing the best combination of the old and the new, and the most versatility in rig. It's no wonder that the type became so popular.

The sloop rig is lofty, indeed, with double spreaders, and sports both a permanent backstay and lower runners. The jib is self-tending for ease of handling, and the deck layout is clean and simple. The yawl rig carried more sail area, though that of the main is reduced by the presence of the mizzen. With a single set of spreaders, the shrouds are more simply arranged, and it's interesting that Aage Nielsen, who drew up the sail plan, included lazyjacks for all the sails. It was obviously a well-thought-out rig for the singlehander, yet designed to achieve good performance.

Construction is sturdy and straightforward, designed to make the best use of materials, and go together without complications. Two different cabin trunk configurations (with the forward end either bent round or squared off) are provided, as are two different accommodations plans—a three-berth arrangement with galley amidships, and a four-berth arrangement with galley forward. Both offer simple, spacious treatments and would be hard to improve upon.

This version of the Malabar Jr. series represents one of the earliest efforts at combining the best attributes of traditional working craft with the state of the art (at the time) in rig design and cruising accommodations. For us, it is a timeless example which ought to grace our waters again.

The plans are moderately detailed, suited for the boatbuilder of experience, and include two sail plans, lines, offsets, construction plans, two cabin plans, yawl rig construction modification, specifications, and two block lists. Price for the set is $150.

Plan 4

DESCRIPTION

Hull type: Round-bottomed, outside-ballasted keel boat

Rig: Marconi sloop or yawl

Construction: Carvel-planked over steamed frames

Headroom/cabin (between beams):   About 5'3"

Featured in Design Section: WB No. 41

PERFORMANCE

*Suitable for: Open ocean

*Intended capacity: 3-8 daysailing, 3 cruising

Trailerable: With difficulty; permit required

Propulsion: Sail w/auxiliary

Speed (knots):   3-7

BUILDING DATA

Skill needed: Advanced

Lofting required: Yes

*Alternative construction: Cold-molded, strip

PLANS DATA

No. of sheets: 7

Level of detail: Average

Cost per set: $150.00

WB Plan No. 4

* *See page 112 for further information.*

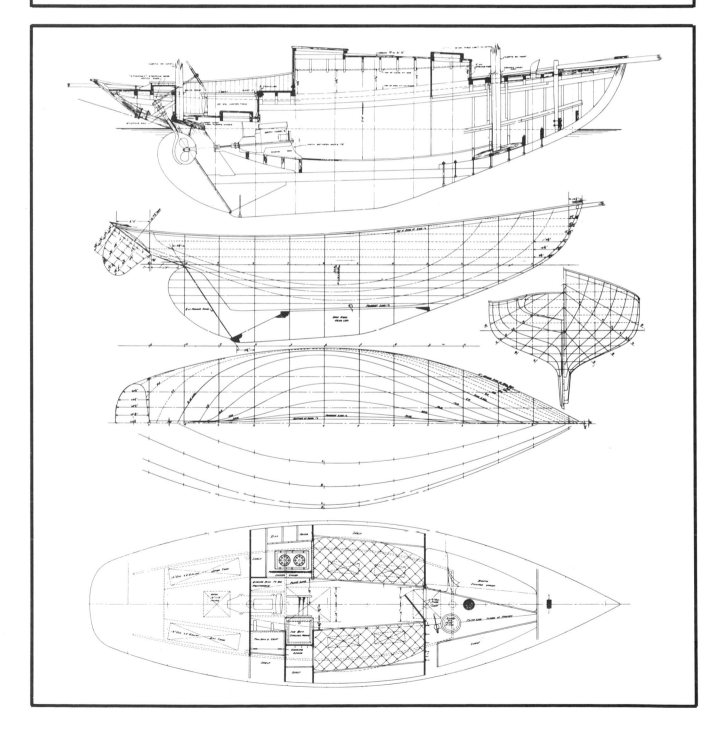

30'4" Keel/Centerboard Sloop

by John G. Alden

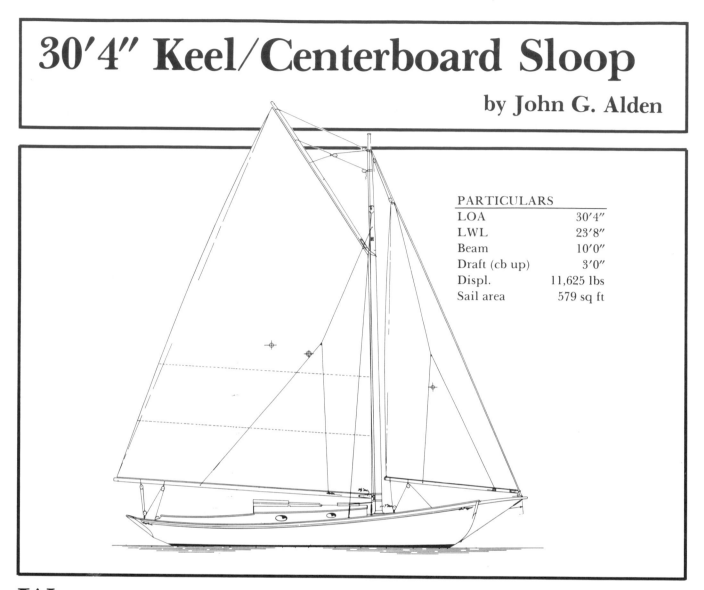

PARTICULARS

LOA	30'4"
LWL	23'8"
Beam	10'0"
Draft (cb up)	3'0"
Displ.	11,625 lbs
Sail area	579 sq ft

When this auxiliary cruiser was designed in 1926, the contemporary yachting press was busy publishing letters and essays on the pros and cons of keel vs. centerboard cruising boats. Though the discussion raged on for months, and though the remarkable performance of centerboard craft at sea was well documented by a number of men of tremendous experience, there was always the sense that the lovers of deep-keel craft were simply greater in number. And in those days there was plenty of deep water to go around.

Times have changed in this last half century. The crowded harbors have caused the modern cruiser to search for thinner water, where fewer boats will go. So, if you like the look and feel of the Malabar Jr. (WB Plan No. 4) but require a board-up draft of no more than 3', this boat deserves a very close look. She is wholesome, with a simple rig, simple accommodations, and a wonderfully traditional look.

Though her sail plan is tall, it is not as tall as it would have to be were it marconi-rigged, and not as complicated either, as it would be with the additional shrouds and stays required. In fact, she'd make a fine little singlehander with her self-tending jib, aft-leading upper and lower shrouds (no backstays), and main and jib lazyjacks.

Her lines provide an interesting combination of elements: hollow entrance, slowly rising run to the buttocks, and very firm bilges. Those elements should combine to make her weatherly, fast, and stiff. In addition, she is a most

pleasing shape to behold in profile and plan. (But what else would we expect from Fenwick Williams, who drew her?)

Accommodations are limited in this plan to three,. although other layouts could be devised without much trouble. The forward cabin is separate from the main cabin, and it contains the head. The offset companionway ladder gives the cook plenty of room, and the layout of compartments and lockers is simple and straightforward. It has to be, for this is a cruiser with under 5' of headroom. The two hatch openings will provide good ventilation, however, as well as two means of escape in case of a fire below decks.

Her construction is rugged and simple, and though there isn't a considerable amount of detail in the plan, there is plenty for a builder with experience. In any case, the scantlings present no problem as far as materials go, and a fine boat would result. A 3,200-pound cast-iron ballast keel is specified, and some inside trimming ballast in the form of lead pigs would be required as well. The self-draining cockpit is really a large footwell, in that the seating is on the bridge- and afterdecks, and no cockpit seats are drawn in.

As a matter of fact, the more one studies this little craft, the more one realizes that she embodies the whole spirit of yachting as it was once meant to be, and perhaps should be again.

Plans consist of lines, offsets, sail plan, construction, cabin plan, block list, and specifications. WB Plan No. 7. $135.00.

Plan 7

DESCRIPTION

Hull type: Round-bottomed, outside-ballasted keel/cb boat

Rig: Gaff sloop

Construction: Carvel planked over steamed frames

Headroom/cabin (between beams):   About 4'7"

Featured in Design Section: WB No. 42

PERFORMANCE

*Suitable for: Open ocean

*Intended capacity: 3-8 daysailing, 3 cruising

Trailerable: With difficulty; permit required

Propulsion: Sail w/auxiliary

Speed (knots): 3-7

BUILDING DATA:

Skill needed: Advanced

Lofting required: Yes

*Alternative construction: Cold-molded, strip

PLANS DATA

No. of sheets: 4

Level of detail: Average

Cost per set: $135.00

WB Plan No. 7

See page 112 for further information.

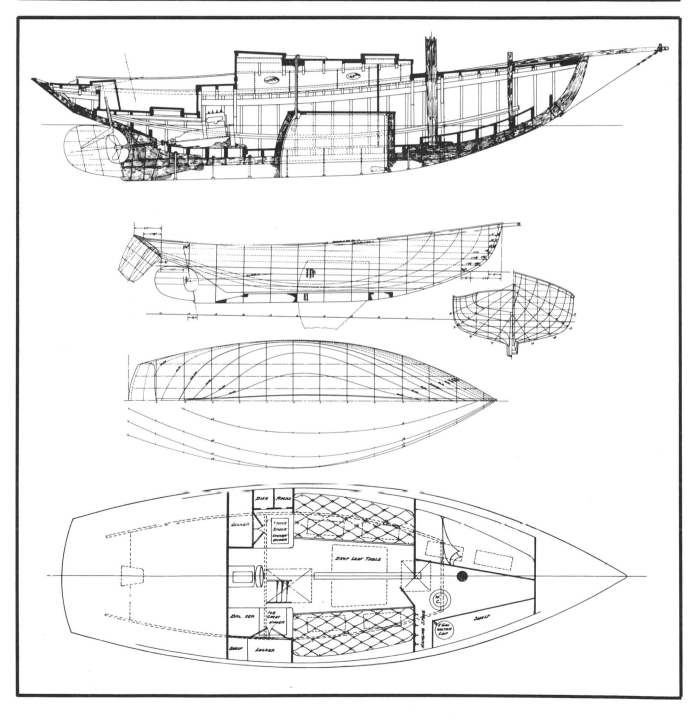

31'3" Concordia Sloop

by Concordia Company

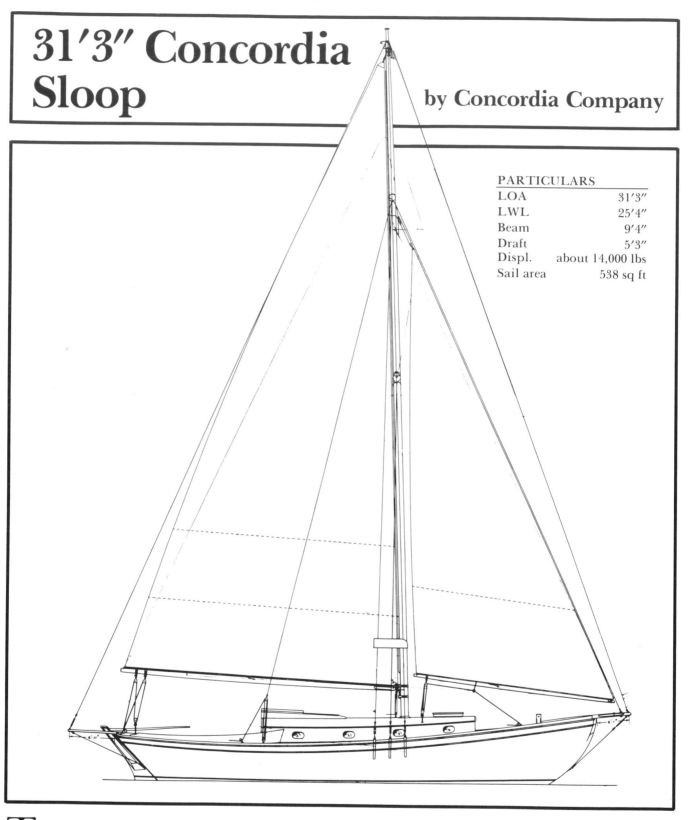

PARTICULARS

LOA	31'3"
LWL	25'4"
Beam	9'4"
Draft	5'3"
Displ.	about 14,000 lbs
Sail area	538 sq ft

The Concordia "31s" are exceedingly practical and well-thought-out boats, and a great many of their features later appeared in the famous Concordia yawls. The "31s" were never intended to be as fancy, though, and experience has shown that workboat construction standards and paint schemes look right at home on these craft.

This cruiser is a step up from the Concordia "28" and was designed to accommodate four in modest comfort. Her mainsail and single jib sail plan, absence of complicated deck fittings, good working deck space, and self-bailing cockpit make her a joy to sail. Her wide companionway hatch leads to a spacious cabin, with galley arranged on either side of the ladder, special Concordia fold-back berth/seats amidships, and two V-berths and head forward. Her locker space has been planned carefully for utmost utility and includes a hanging locker, transom lockers, and a bureau for linens and extra blankets.

The plans, consisting of 11 sheets, include lines, offsets, sail plan, arrangement plan, and construction plan. WB Plan No. 33. $150.00.

Plan 33

DESCRIPTION
Hull type: Round-bottomed with outside ballast keel
Rig: Marconi sloop
Construction: Carvel planked over steamed frames
Headroom/cabin (between beams): About 5'10"
Featured in Design Section: WB No. 48

PERFORMANCE
*Suitable for: Open ocean

*Intended capacity: 3-8 daysailing, 4 cruising
Trailerable: With difficulty; permit required
Propulsion: Sail w/auxiliary inboard engine
Speed (knots): 3-7

BUILDING DATA
Skill needed: Advanced
Lofting required: Yes
*Alternative construction: Cold-molded, strip

PLANS DATA
No. of sheets: 11
Level of detail: Average
Cost per set: $150.00
WB Plan No. 33

See page 112 for further information.

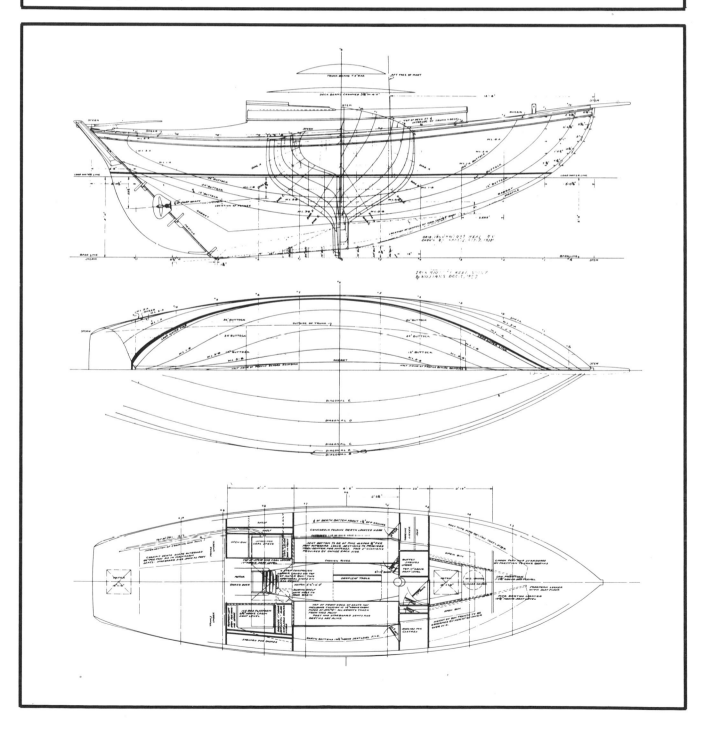

32'5" Sharpie Ketch, Two Lucys

by Robert Beebe

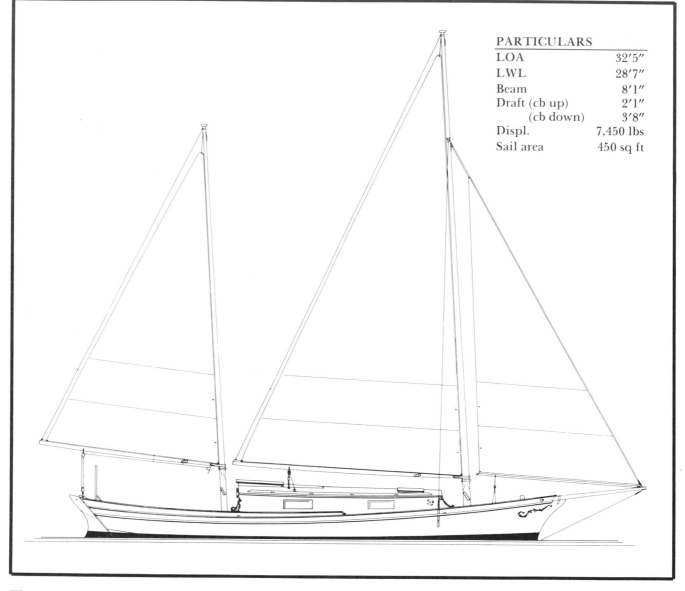

PARTICULARS	
LOA	32'5"
LWL	28'7"
Beam	8'1"
Draft (cb up)	2'1"
(cb down)	3'8"
Displ.	7,450 lbs
Sail area	450 sq ft

Low cost, ease of building, and shallow draft have quite rightly made the sailing sharpie a long-time favorite. Here's an unusually well-thought-out sharpie with some special features that make her a good cruiser. Since lack of space in the cabin has been the common complaint with sharpies because of their shallow hulls and low freeboard, this boat's cabin sides have been brought outboard to be flush with her rails, giving people in the cabin comfortable sitting headroom all the way out to the sides of the hull. The centerboard trunk is further forward than usual, leaving the galley area in the after part of the cabin unobstructed. Because of her V-bottom cross-planked construction, bottom framing is virtually eliminated and the cabin sole can be kept low—in fact, it rests directly on top of the inner keel. The combination of the low cabin sole and the high-as-it-can-be-and-not-look-bad cabintop, gives unusual, although by no means full, headroom below. Her cabin is laid out to sleep three and to comfortably sit several more.

The deck aft of the cabin has been kept level, rather than sheered, for practical use as a place to lounge or sleep in the open. At other times it is, of course, where you can sit to sail or simply enjoy being outside.

We're told by her designer that this boat sails well and balances nicely. With her half ton of outside lead ballast, long hull lines, and a well-proportioned marconi ketch rig, we can see why. As a low-cost, easily cared-for, protected-water cruiser—one well within reach of an amateur builder—this sharpie would be nearly perfect.

The plans come in seven sheets, and include lines and offsets, construction, motor installation and cabin plan, sail plan, and details for spars, tangs, and wooden fittings. WB Plan No. 55. $75.00.

Plan 55

DESCRIPTION
Hull type: V-bottomed centerboard sharpie
Rig: Marconi ketch
Construction: Carvel-planked sides over sawn frames; cross-planked bottom
Headroom/cabin (between beams):   About 4′5″

PERFORMANCE
*Suitable for: Somewhat protected waters
*Intended capacity: 6 daysailing, 3 cruising

* *See page 112 for further information.*

Trailerable: With difficulty, permit required
Propulsion: Sail w/auxiliary inboard engine
Speed (knots):   3-6

BUILDING DATA:
Skill needed: Intermediate
Lofting required: Yes
*Alternative construction: Strip-planked topsides

PLANS DATA
No. of sheets: 7
Level of detail: Average
Cost per set: $75.00
WB Plan No. 55

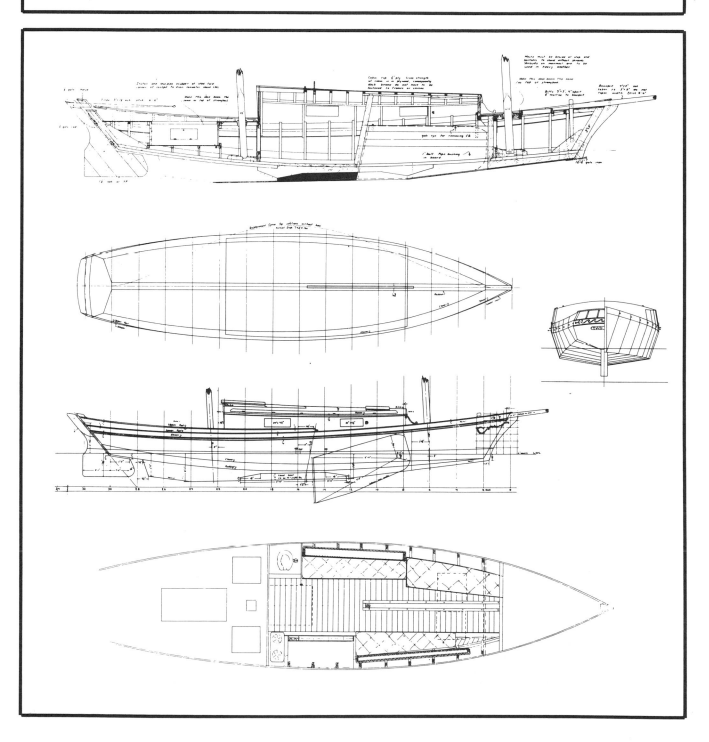

33'4" Concordia Sloop

by Concordia Company

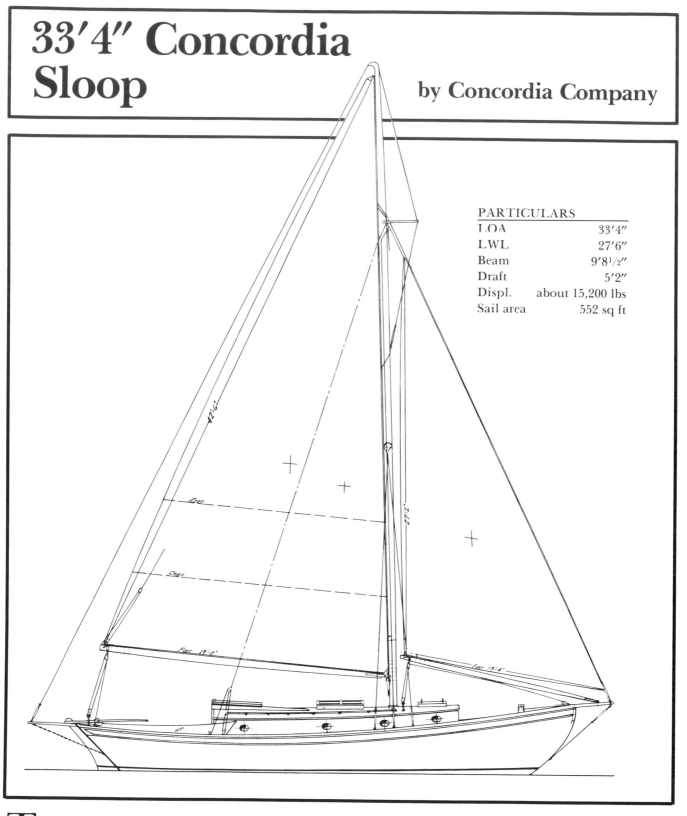

PARTICULARS	
LOA	33'4"
LWL	27'6"
Beam	9'8½"
Draft	5'2"
Displ.	about 15,200 lbs
Sail area	552 sq ft

The Concordia "33" is a lovely boat that is bigger, more graceful, and faster than her earlier sisters. She has a good, roomy cockpit, standing headroom under the deckhouse, two cabins, and an enclosed head. Like the other Concordias, she features a clean deck arrangement, an uncomplicated rig, and an honest, frill-less appearance. With a club-footed jib and a well-proportioned mainsail, she is very easy to handle. (See WB No. 48.)

For a full-keel traditional boat, she is surprisingly easily driven, and frequently sails by more modern boats of her length in moderate winds. Her interior is spacious enough to allow for considerable variation on the standard layout— from spartan to elegant.

The overall length of this able cruiser is 33'4", which is long enough to carry a pretty sheer and allow pleasing proportions of the bow and stern. This is a delightful, comfortable, and amazingly fast boat for cruising with two couples or an entire family.

Plans, with five sheets, consist of lines, offsets, arrangment, sail, and construction plans. WB Plan No. 34. $150.00.

Plan 34

DESCRIPTION
Hull type: Round-bottomed with outside ballast keel
Rig: Marconi sloop
Construction: Carvel planked over steamed frames
Headroom/cabin (between beams): about 6'3"
Featured in Design Section: WB No. 48

PERFORMANCE
*Suitable for: Open ocean

* See page 112 for further information.

*Intended capacity: 3-8 daysailing, 4 cruising
Trailerable: With difficulty; permit required
Propulsion: Sail w/auxiliary inboard engine
Speed (knots): 3-7

BUILDING DATA
Skill needed: Advanced
Lofting required: Yes
*Alternative construction: Cold-molded, strip

PLANS DATA
No. of sheets: 5
Level of detail: Average
Cost per set: $150.00
WB Plan No. 34

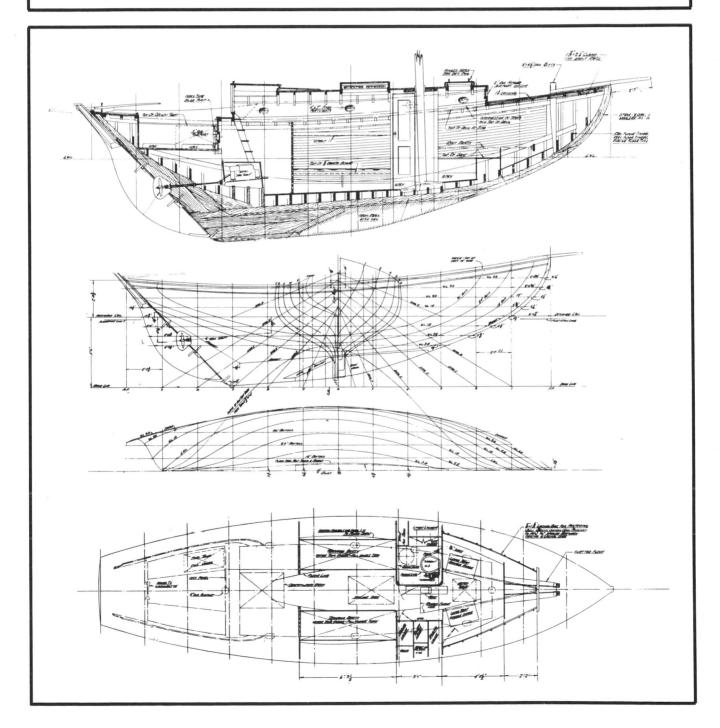

35′ Cruising Ketch/Cutter

by Charles Wittholz

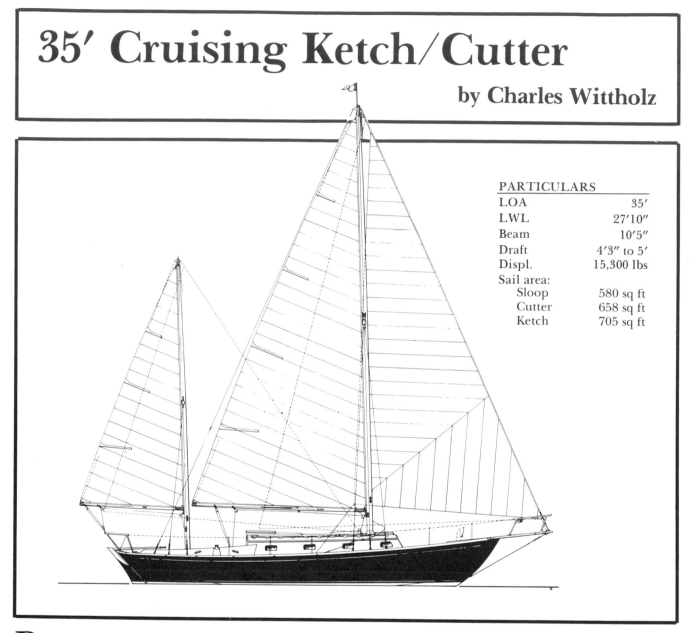

PARTICULARS	
LOA	35′
LWL	27′10″
Beam	10′5″
Draft	4′3″ to 5′
Displ.	15,300 lbs
Sail area:	
Sloop	580 sq ft
Cutter	658 sq ft
Ketch	705 sq ft

Because she was designed to be built in large numbers as a stock boat where the selling price was very much a consideration, this so-called Departure Class cruiser's plans have been unusually well thought out for efficient building. The Dickerson yard near Cambridge, Maryland, turned out a lot of these boats in the late 1950s and early '60s, and many sets of plans have been sold to others directly by the designer since then. As a result, both the boat herself and the plans for her have proven themselves as more than adequate.

She's a relatively easily built V-bottomed chine boat that is set up on and planked over her sawn oak frames; there's no steam-bending required and, if boat lumber is hard to get in your part of the world, her planking can be of sheet plywood installed according to the alternate construction plan for that material. In spite of her simple construction (its chief disadvantage is the somewhat boxy look common to most V-bottomed hulls), she compares favorably with more expensive round-bilged hulls in performance and cabin space. She's sharp enough forward not to pound in a sea, heavy enough to be seakindly, and her sailing lines are long enough to allow her to drive along easily under sail.

Inside, she has the layout that has worked so well for most 35′ cruising boats over the years—a forward cabin with V-berths for two, an enclosed "head" to port and lockers to starboard just aft of the forward cabin, followed by the main cabin with two settee berths (with space over them for two upper berths if cruising with six people is a necessity), and a full-width galley area aft near the companionway. Best of all, there's full headroom the whole length of the cabin. For convenience and safety, her cockpit is self-bailing. The cockpit area is big, however, and there's room for 8-10 persons while daysailing. Size for size, it would be hard to find more real boat for the money.

As with many well-used and well-loved designs, there are a number of options shown on the drawings that have been developed over the years. For better seakeeping, there are lines for a deeper, 5′-draft hull. You can take your choice of lead or iron for ballast keel casting, and there are plans for fitting her with an aft cabin and inboard rudder. There are also plans for rigging her as a sloop, a cutter, or for adding a bowsprit to the standard ketch rig—a recommendation of the designer. The plans come in 15 sheets, and besides the above options, they show lines and offsets for ketch or sloop, arrangement and construction, main deck plan, rigging details, plywood planking and joinerwork details. WB Plan No. 49. $300.00.

Plan 49

DESCRIPTION
Hull type: V-bottomed, outside-ballasted keel boat
Rig: Ketch, cutter, or sloop
Construction: Carvel planked over sawn frames
Headroom/cabin (between beams):   About 6'4"

PERFORMANCE
*Suitable for: Open ocean
*Intended capacity: 8-10 daysailing, 4-6 cruising

* See page 112 for further information.

Trailerable: No
Propulsion: Sail w/auxiliary
Speed (knots):   3-7

BUILDING DATA:
Skill needed: Advanced
Lofting required: Yes
*Alternative construction: Plywood (plans included)

PLANS DATA
No. of sheets: 15
Level of detail: Above average
Cost per set: $300.00
WB Plan No. 49

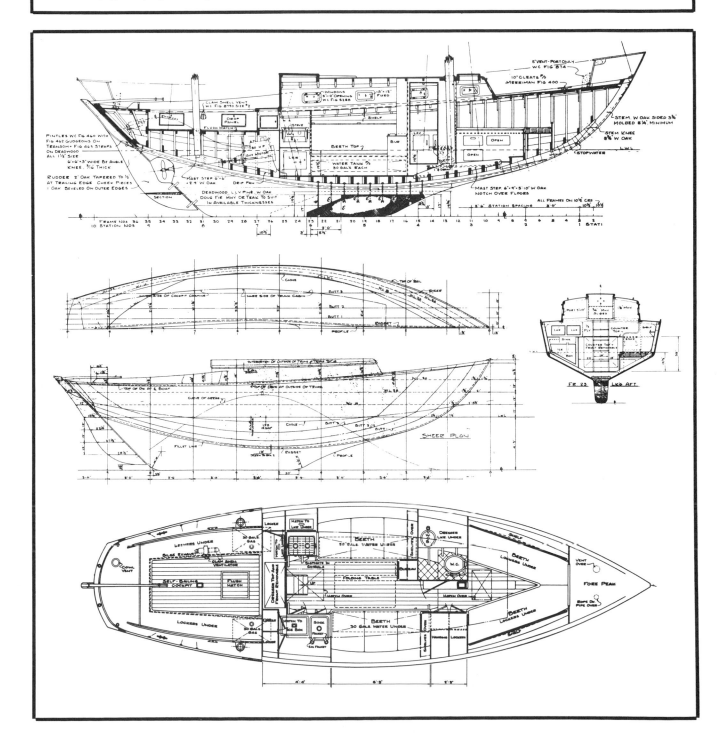

41'3" Schooner, Malabar II

by John G. Alden

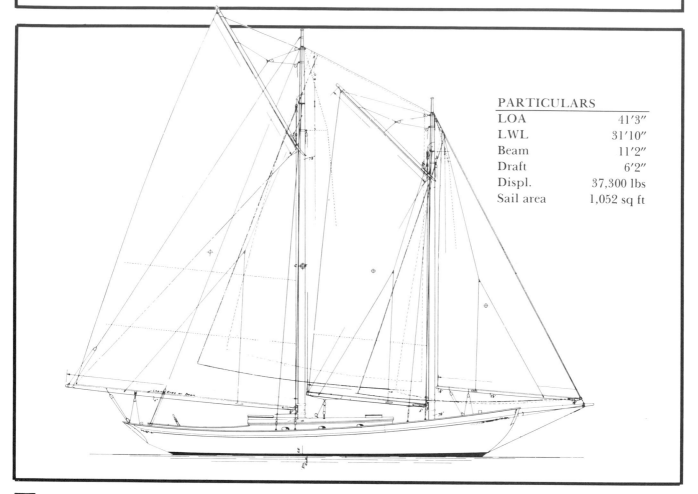

PARTICULARS	
LOA	41'3"
LWL	31'10"
Beam	11'2"
Draft	6'2"
Displ.	37,300 lbs
Sail area	1,052 sq ft

Few rigs charm the hearts of sailors as much as the schooner, and John Alden knew how to design cruising schooners that were fast and able, dry and comfortable. In the first three Malabars (WB No. 32), Alden was striving not only for these qualities, but for a simplicity of rig that would allow the small schooners to be sailed singlehanded by none other than himself, for the boats of that name were all designed and built for himself. Yet, it is Malabar II that appeals to us most—both in outward appearance, with her single, small deckhouse, and in accommodation, which is simple and symmetrical. The later Malabars were bigger and much more sophisticated boats which in turn required considerably more money to keep them going.

What the designer wanted was a cruising boat in which he could go anywhere on- or offshore, which would stay at sea in almost any weather, and yet would not be too much to handle alone. Although the Malabars performed remarkably well under racing conditions, Alden wanted anything but a racing machine, with its high angle of heel and constantly straining hull and rig. Her generous freeboard and high sheer forward made the Malabar as dry a boat as a sailor could want.

As for the rig of Malabar II, it was very simple. The sails were sheeted to travelers, making them all self-tending when tacking. Lazyjacks were rigged on all the sails, and the foremast was stepped well forward so as to keep the jib small enough to handle comfortably. John Alden noted that Malabar II would beat to weather under foresail alone, and would "move along well in light weather." It was the efficiency of this rig, in combination with the carefully worked out lines, that made Malabar II unique.

The construction of the schooner is stout but simple, worked out, we feel certain, in collaboration with Charles Morse of Thomaston, Maine, her builder. She was said to have endured extremely well, and failed to show any signs of weakening under the stresses of considerable sailing. She was, in fact, a remarkable combination of wisdom and experience on the part of both designer and builder. She is still going strong, with a new hull built in the mid-'50s. Shortly afterward she made a successful transatlantic passage, and now hails from Martha's Vineyard, Massachusetts.

As part of our continuing effort to make some of John Alden's work available, and to encourage the building of fine boats, we are pleased to present one of Alden's finest. The plans are moderately detailed, and this is not a boat for amateur construction. It is, however, an extraordinary example of a fine cruising schooner, and well worth careful study. Drawings consist of sail plan, lines, offsets, construction, deck construction, cabin plan, iron keel plan, specifications, and block list. WB Plan No. 8. $850.00.

Plan 8

DESCRIPTION

Hull type: Round-bottomed, outside-ballasted
   keel boat

Rig: Gaff schooner

Construction: Carvel planked over steamed frames

Headroom/cabin (between beams):   about 6'2"

Featured in Design Section: WB No. 41

PERFORMANCE

*Suitable for: Open ocean

*Intended capacity: 4-10 daysailing, 6 cruising

See page 112 for further information.

Trailerable: No

Propulsion: Sail w/auxiliary

Speed (knots):   3-8

BUILDING DATA:

Skill needed: Advanced

Lofting required: Yes

*Alternative construction: None

PLANS DATA

No. of sheets: 5

Level of details: Average

Cost per set: $850.00**

WB Plan No. 8

*** Price changed in 1990 at request of John G. Alden, Inc.*

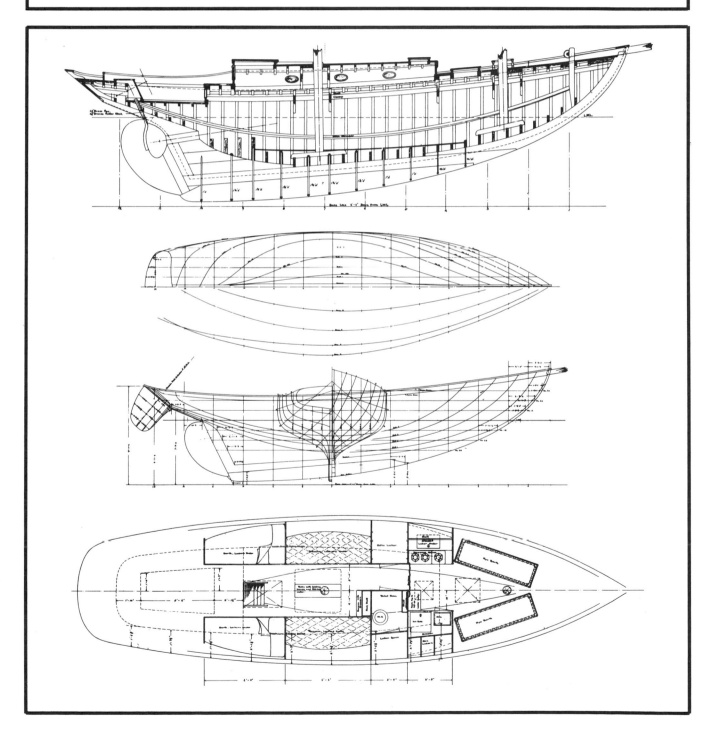

Try these other good books from WoodenBoat. You'll find titles on boatbuilding, design, repair, woodworking, and nautical history.

Fifty Wooden Boats
A Catalog of Study Plans

The first in the series, this book contains study plans for 50 designs—which range from a 7′ 7″ pram to a 41′ 3″ schooner. There are 5 tenders and prams, 7 sailing dinghies and pulling boats, 4 performance rowing craft, 3 power cruisers, 9 daysailers, and 22 cruisers. In addition there are drawings that identify the parts of a wooden boat, a bibliography, a guide for the selection of various woods, and instructions by Weston Farmer on reading boat plans. None of the designs are repeated in these three books. Some of the most frugal folks we know (the kind that weigh the various loaves of breads on the scale, to select just the right loaf) still can't believe what a great value these are.

112 pp., softcover
#325-060 Ship Wt. 1 lb $12.95

Thirty Wooden Boats
A Second Catalog of Study Plans

These 30 designs include: 6 powerboats, 6 daysailers, 11 cruising boats, 2 canoes, a kayak, and 4 small sailing/pulling boats. Also included is an article by designer Joel White on understanding boat plans.

80 pp., softcover
#325-061 Ship Wt. 1 lb $12.95

Forty Wooden Boats
A Third Catalog of Study Plans

These are the newest designs added to WoodenBoat's collection since the publication of *Fifty Wooden Boats* and *Thirty Wooden Boats*. These popular books contain details usually found with study plans: hull dimensions, displacement, sail area, construction methods and the degree of boatbuilding skill needed to complete each project. Some of the 40 designs include L. Francis Herreshoff's *Rozinante*, Brewer's Mystic Sharpie, 5 kayaks built using a variety of methods (including a double kayak), a canoe, 2 peapods, a catamaran, daysailers, a single and double rowing shell, skiffs, mahogany runabouts, and many more.

96 pp., softcover
325-062 Ship Wt. 1 lb $12.95

Designer & Client
Eight Boat Design Commissions— from Kayak to Cruiser
by Antonio Dias

Boat design is one of those things we should all dabble in. Be it on a scrap of paper, or in the margins of your lecture/meeting notes. After you read this book, you'll find those doodles looking pretty good, and the revised doodles looking great. Why? Because of what you will learn by following the give-and-take process between naval architect Tony Dias and eight different boat-savvy client. Each client has their own ideal boat in their mind's eye. You get to spectate as the desires and realities unfold.

150 pp., softcover
#325-113 Ship Wt. 2 lbs $22.95

William Fife
Master of the Classic Yacht
by Franco Pace

What a combination: the vintage yachts of William Fife as photographed by Franco Pace, one of the top nautical photographers in the world. Hundreds of lush photographs, including full-page and full-spread shots. Featuring close-up details of sailors just managing to stay onboard, overhead shots in water clear enough to see an entire keel, plus racing and playing in the Mediterranean. Keep this by your bedside, or on your end table because looking at beautiful images of exceptional boats is good for the soul, and is bound to lower your blood pressure.
Nineteen different Fife boats are featured including *Altair, Belle Aventure, Moonbeam, Pen Duick, Tuiga, Dione, Fulmar, Halloween, Tonino, Yvette, Clio, Merry Dancer, Kentra, Sumurun, Mariella, Cintra, Flica II, Solway Maid, Osborne.*

160 pp., hardcover, includes protective slipcase
#325-112 Ship Wt. 3 lbs $69.95

Building Small Boats
by Greg Rössel

For years Greg has been teaching the fundamentals here at our WoodenBoat School. Greg's talent for relaying this experience into the written word has resulted in a text with a straight-forward friendly approach, including helpful drawings and photographs. The combination will drive-home the lessons. *Building Small Boats* is the ideal book for the construction of boats under 25 feet in length. It's perfect for folks looking to have some of the mysteries of the building process peeled away, or just boning-up on a good technique or two.
Chapters include: A Boat and a Shop to Build It In; Tools; Homemade Tools; Wood for Boatbuilding; Fastenings; Glues, Paints, and Potions; Lofting Demystified; The Stem; The Keel; The Molds and Transom; The Setup; The Art of Bending Frames; Lining Off the Hull; Planking Stock; Carvel Planking; Lapstrake Planking; Centerboard, Centerboard Trunk, and Rudder; Stiffening the Hull; Interior Work; The Deck; Solid Wood Spars; What Looks Good?; The Builder's Half Model; plus Glossary/Sources/Tables.

278 pp., hardcover
#325-111 Ship Wt. 4 lbs $39.95

How to Build a Wooden Boat
by David C. "Bud" McIntosh
Illustrated by Samuel F. Manning

Here is everything you need to know to construct a carvel planked cruising boat with no more than a set of plans, a pile of lumber, and determination. Written and illustrated by experienced boatbuilders, this book covers the entire process, from lofting to finishing out. Setting up molds, lining off, ribbands, steaming and fitting frames, planking, pouring the keel, bulkheads and floorboards, decks, rudders, spars—the works.

254 pp., hardcover
#325-075 Ship Wt. 2 1/2 lbs $36.00

Lofting
by Allan H. Vaitses

Lofting is the process of drawing lines of a boat full-size, to get the shapes and patterns needed for building. You take the numbers from the offset table, plot them on the floor, and then play connect the dots. Okay, it's not *that* simple. If it were, you wouldn't need the book. First published in the 1980s and out of print far too long, *Lofting* is that one-stop shopping for filling your void of this particular knowledge base. Because lofting is such a foundation element of boatbuilding, you really should understand how to do it. And while this topic has probably scared-off more folks from building than any other reason, fear not.

150 pp., softcover with wire-o binding for easy shop use
#325-114 Ship Wt. 2 lbs $19.95

How to Build the Catspaw Dinghy
by the Editors of WoodenBoat

A detailed manual on the building of a superior rowing and sailing dinghy. A modified version (carvel instead of lapstrake planking) of the famous Herreshoff Columbia dinghy, this measures 12′ 8″, and makes an excellent project for the boatbuilder with intermediate skills. While offsets are included with this book, working from the plans is recommended.

32 pp., softcover
#325-010 Ship Wt. 1/2 lb $8.95

How to Build the Gloucester Light Dory
by Harold H. Payson

A shop manual on building an exceptional rowing dory. Designed by Philip C. Bolger, the 15′ 6″ Gloucester Light Dory is fast, seaworthy, and a delight to row. Author and builder "Dynamite" Payson has built hundreds of these. It features simple plywood construction. Includes a full set of reduced plans, as well as step-by-step photos plus sketches of how to set-up.

32 pp., softcover
#325-005 Ship Wt. 1/2 lb $7.95

The Dory Model Book
by Harold "Dynamite" Payson

It's model building time, and Dynamite is just the person to show you how. Three traditional Down East boats are featured: a Banks dory (19″ long), a Friendship dory (27 1/2″ long) and a Friendship dory skiff (18″ long). All models are based on authentic boats and built the same way the full-sized boats are built. Step-by-step instructions, along with materials lists, as well as how to build a display case for the beautiful outcome of your labors. Plus there are pages of modeling tips that will help with this project as well as any other models you build. Be prepared for an addictive process.

84 pp., zillions of photos., softcover
#325-109 Ship Wt. 1 lb $19.95

KayakCraft
Fine Woodstrip Kayak Construction

by Ted Moores

Combine the designing talent of naval architect Steve Killing with the experience and finesse of builder Ted Moores, and you are on the way to creating an exquisite small craft.

Even if you have built a strip canoe, you'll want this book for the designs as well as the additional techniques for the making the cockpit coaming, hatches, and decking. And if you already have some of the building skills, getting the low-down from a builder whose work hangs in museums is likely to improve your own technique a notch or two. While the popular 17' *Endeavour* kayak is the boat used throughout the book, *KayakCraft* also gives you lines and offsets for three other Steve Killing designed kayaks: a 14' sport kayak, a 16' 6" touring kayak, and a 20' 6" tandem kayak. Just apply the same techniques to build the boat that best suits your needs.If you are a first-time builder, you'll be amazed at the building and paddling rewards in store for you.

185 pp., softcover
#325-115 Ship Wt. 2 lbs **$19.95**

Featherweight Boatbuilding

by Henry "Mac" McCarthy

It is Mac's mission to open your eyes to the natural beauty around you. He does so by providing this course to create and use an ideal double-paddle canoe. The Wee Lassie is practical and beautiful, lightweight and strong, and will carry you to waterways that are inaccessible in most boats. Mac draws on years of experience teaching hundreds of people in his shop, and at our WoodenBoat School here in Maine. The Wee Lassie is strip-built, an especially forgiving building technique for the first-time builder. This book contains everything you need to build—step-by-step photographs, clear text, diagrams, plans—and inspiration.

96 pp., softcover
#325-104 Ship Wt. 1 lb **$19.95**

Traditional Boatbuilding Made Easy
Building Heidi

by Richard Kolin

This is wooden boat building at its most pleasurable—a 12' skiff done in the traditional manner—solid planking, copper clench nails, bronze fittings, three-strand rope, the aroma of cedar planking, turps, penetrating oils, and marine paint. Rich's clear drawings and text make this the ideal way to get into traditional construction.

84 pp., softcover
#325-103 Ship Wt. 1 lb **$19.95**

How to Build the Shellback Dinghy

by Eric Dow

Construct this 11' 2" dinghy following the step-by-step instructions of builder Eric Dow. The Shellback Dinghy is a modern classic that rows, tows, and sails beautifully. She has a traditional bow, a narrow rockered bottom, and a sweet transom that lifts well out of the water. Everything has been engineered with the amateur builder in mind.

64 pp., softcover
#325-040 Ship Wt. 1/2 lb **$15.00**

How to Build the Haven 12 ½-Footer

by Maynard Bray

This is Joel White's keel/centerboard variation of the famous Herreshoff 12½. Each step in this unique process is carefully explained and illustrated. This book, in combination with detailed construction plans, provides a thorough guide for advanced amateurs. No lofting is required.

64 pp., softcover
#325-077 Ship Wt. 1/2 lb **$15.00**

Building the Nutshell Pram

by Maynard Bray

A step-by-step construction manual for this very popular Joel White design, for oar and sail. Part of the popularity is due to the ease of construction, especially the bow. This instruction book is beneficial for anyone who wishes to build the pram from scratch using WoodenBoat's full-scale plans.

32 pp., softcover, #325-035 Ship Wt. 1/2 lb **$7.95**

The WoodenBoat Series

Painting & Varnishing

Painting and varnishing is part art and part science. No matter the standard of finish— utilitarian through show quality and anything in between—the keys to success are a well-conceived plan of action, the correct choice of tools and materials, a careful preparation of the surface, proper application of the coating, and a "feel" for what you are doing. This book contains twenty-four articles from *WoodenBoat* magazine including Stripping Old Paint, Dealing With Mildew, Scrapers, Water-Based Clear Coatings, Antifouling Paints, Paintbrush Care, Mast Protection, Quick Tips to Springtime Varnishing and Painting, Linear Polyurethanes, Paint Adhesion, and more. Have this by your side when you are planning your boat's finishing touches.

146 pp., softcover, #325-101 Ship Wt. 2 lbs **$22.95**

10 Wooden Boats You Can Build
For Sail, Power, Oar and Paddle

The beauty of this book is that the construction bugs have already been worked out of the designs. Plans, step-by-step building instructions, materials lists, clear photographs, and detailed diagrams are included; every boat was built before the plans and instructions were published. Many, like the Cartopper, the Flat-Bottomed Skiff, the Cape Charles, and the Wee Lassie, have been built by the hundreds. Follow the building process for a variety of designs: a Herreshoff Daysailer, a Lapstrake Plywood Runabout, a Norwegian Pram, a Strip-Built Double-Paddle Canoe, a Cold-Molded Dinghy, a Bateau, and a Double-Paddle Lapstrake Sailing Canoe.

196 pp., softcover, #325-102 Ship Wt. 2 lbs **$24.95**

25 Woodworking Projects
For Small and Large Boats

Projects for the novice and expert. Projects for the shop or on board. Projects for anyone wanting to fulfill their nautical desires. Here are the best woodworking projects shown in *WoodenBoat* magazine. They range from a simple bailer, to a stunning ship's wheel. And in between are oars, single and double-bladed paddles, louvered doors, an icebox, a skylight, hollow spars, and much more.Every project was written by people who have actually made what they are writing about.

198 pp., softcover, #325-107 Ship Wt. 2 lbs **$22.95**

100 Boat Designs Reviewed
Design Commentaries by the Experts

With this book in hand, you will hold the collective wisdom of the ages. Or at least the wisdom of the experts. A mountain of information has been culled from the best boat design reviews from *WoodenBoat* magazine. You'll spend hours pouring over a variety of boats, from rowing craft to powerboats, daysailers to cruising boats. The reviews are comprehensive and thorough. No once-over-lightly here. There is an analysis of the lines, construction plan, accommodation plan, plus recommendations for improvements. The scope of work includes designs by John Alden, Joel White, Henry Scheel, Howard Chapelle, S.S. Crocker, and many others. This is a wonderful book for boat dreamers. Study these plans, read these commentaries, go sailing in your mind.

264 pp., softcover, #325-108 Ship Wt. 2 ½ lbs **$24.95**

Planking & Fastening

Perhaps the most satisfying task in wooden boat building is planking, as this is the point when all the planning that went into the boat bears fruit. Finally, all the elements are here—the flowing lines, the lovely sheer, the enclosed space. Now it looks like a boat. Gathered here is the information necessary for preparing to plank, clamping the planks in place, fastening the planks to the structure, and finishing off. The advice is based on actual projects, some large, some small; the advisors are all expert wooden boatbuilders. This book is a gold mine of information that will help and encourage readers with the building of a new boat or the repair of an old one.

170 pp., softcover, #325-106 Ship Wt. 2 lbs **$24.95**

Frame, Stem & Keel Repair

The keel, stem, and frames are the very core of wooden boat construction, the elements that provide shape and strength to the structure. They are analogous to the sill, joists, rafters, and framing of a house. If they have integrity, the structure has integrity. If they don't, they must be fixed or the structure will not survive. Here is practical advice from the experts who have done the work themselves. In most cases, they make their points by reviewing a specific project step-by-step, describing why they did what they did, and how they did it. Chapters include: Bending Wood, Designing and Building a Steam Box, Making Laminated Frames, Rebuilding a Centerboard Trunk, and more.

133 pp., softcover, #325-105 Ship Wt. 2 lbs **$24.95**

A Glossary of Wooden Boat Parts

These drawings are of the Sea Bird yawl (WB Plan No. 3) and show the names and locations for each of the important structural members that make up a traditionally built wooden hull. These are the terms that you'll find on most of the plans we sell and are ones that builders and designers (and writers and editors) continuously deal with. If you want to build a boat but don't yet know the names of all its pieces, this might be a good place to start. To be sure, each boat design is a bit different from the others, but after you've mastered what's here, those differences will be easy to learn.

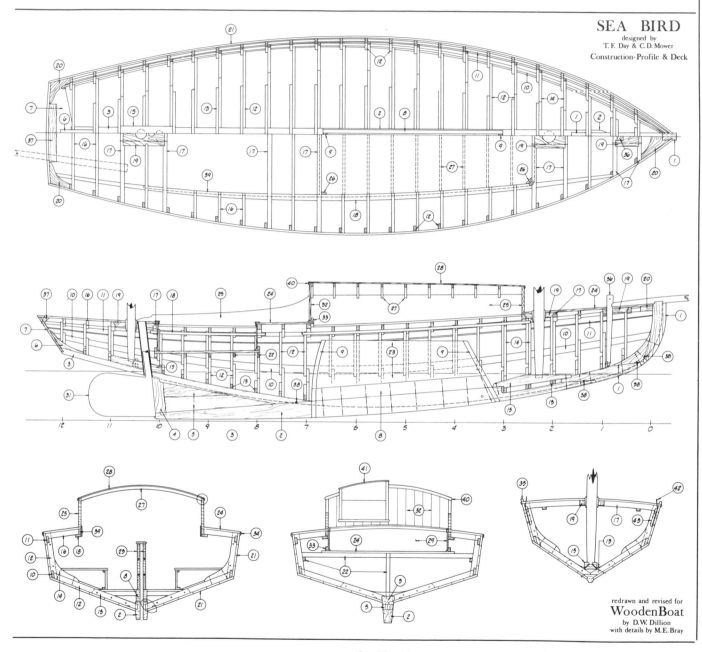

SEA BIRD
designed by
T. F. Day & C. D. Mower
Construction-Profile & Deck

redrawn and revised for
WoodenBoat
by D. W. Dillion
with details by M. E. Bray

Coding for boat parts chart

1. Stem assembly
2. Keel
3. Stern timber
4. Sternpost
5. Deadwood
6. Transom knee
7. Transom
8. Bedlogs
9. Posts at trunk
10. Bilge stringers
11. Sheer clamps
12. Frames
13. Floor timbers
14. Frame knees
15. Mast steps
16. Deckbeams
17. Deckbeams
18. Deck stringers
19. Mast partners & blocking
20. Breasthook & knees
21. Planking
22. Cockpit sole beams & stanchions
23. Centerboard trunk strakes
24. Decking & cockpit sole
25. Coamings, house sides & front
26. House posts
27. House beams
28. Housetop
29. Cockpit staving
30. Centerboard
31. Rudder & stock
32. Aft bulkhead of house
33. Deckhouse & cockpit sills
34. Guardrail
35. Toerail
36. Sampson post
37. Block for boomkins
38. Stopwaters
39. Fillers
40. Molding
41. Companionway
42. Chainplates—main & mizzen
43. Blocking

Guidance on the Selection of Timbers for Constructional Members

SOFTWOODS

Common Name	Notes
balsam fir, eastern fir, Canada balsam, fir	Marginal value in boatbuilding; low durability.
western fir, fir	Sometimes "confused" in the trade with Douglas-fir. Woods are quite different.
incense cedar, pencil cedar, bastard cedar	Often confused with western redcedar. Properties somewhat less desirable for boatbuilding.
Port Orford cedar, Oregon cedar, Lawsons cypress, white cedar	High durability and resistance to acids, superb for decking. Difficult to obtain.
western redcedar, giant arborvitae, canoe cedar, Pacific redcedar	High durability, superb planking timber.
Alaska-cedar, yellow cypress, Alaska yellow-cedar, Sitka cypress, Alaska cypress, Nootka false-cypress	Not to be confused with bald cypress, a wood with quite different properties. High durability and acid resistance; preferred wood for oars, paddles and planking.
northern white-cedar, eastern arborvitae, swamp cedar, eastern white-cedar, post cedar	High durability, superb for cold molding of hulls.
Atlantic white cedar, southern white-cedar, swamp cedar, false cypress	Similar properties to northern white-cedar.
eastern redcedar, closet cedar, red juniper, savin	High durability but not as good as other cedars for boatbuilding.
Pacific yew, western yew, yew	Scarce. Has been used for paddles and oars.
California torreya, California-nutmeg, stinking cedar	Exceptional durability; scarce; has possible boatbuilding uses.
Baldcypress, red cypress, yellow cypress, southern cypress, gulf cypress, white cypress	Not to be confused with Alaska-cedar; high durability and resistance to marine borers. Extensively used in boatbuilding.
redwood, coast redwood, California redwood	High durability and chemical resistance; available in large, clear stock.
Sitka spruce, coast spruce, tide-land spruce, yellow spruce, airplane spruce	Low durability, but very strong for its weight; available in large, clear stock. Used for spars.
white spruce, red spruce, black spruce, Englemann spruce, spruce	Similar to Sitka spruce but clear stock is less common.
tamarack, hackmatack, eastern larch, Alaska larch	Somewhat more decay resistant than spruce; natural crooks favored in boatbuilding.
eastern white pine, northern white pine, Weymouth pine, pumpkin pine, soft pine, white pine	Old-growth heartwood, more decay resistant than second-growth wood.
red pine, Norway pine	Less rot resistant than *Pinus strobus*.
western white pine, Idaho white pine, silver pine, white pine. soft pine	Similar to eastern white pine.
southern yellow pine, southern pine, yellow pine, hard pine, Georgia pine, etc.	More than half a dozen different species; durability ranges from high in old-growth longleaf pine heartwood to poor in second growth of most species.
Douglas-fir, redfir (occasionally yellow-fir, Oregon-pine)	Prized boatbuilding wood, not to be confused with *Abies* spp.
western larch, mountain larch, Montana larch	Harder and heavier than eastern larch.

HARDWOODS

Common Name	Notes
live oak	Extremely durable, once used for ship framing and knees.
white oak, swamp oak, etc.	Several species of white oak varying in decay resistance and strength; many have good strength and durability.
red oak, black oak, gray oak (Maine), etc.	Several species of red oak; collectively less decay resistant than white oak.
elm, white elm, American elm, red elm, hard elm	Several different species of elm, varying in strength properties; all are decay prone.
black locust, shipmast locust, yellow locust	Excellent durability, strength and dimensional stability.
black cherry, cherry	High durability and good dimensional stability.
black walnut, walnut	Similar to cherry.
butternut, white walnut	Hard and light; used for interior trim.
white ash, green or red ash, ash	Tough and easy to bend; not durable.
Oregon ash, ash	Similar to eastern species.
red mulberry	Very durable heartwood; small tree; scarce.
apple	Not durable; occasionally sought for crooks in small craft
sassafrass	Highly durable; has properties like ash but not so tough; once popular in light skiff construction.
Osage orange, bois d'arc, bodark, bowwood, mock orange	Similar to black locust; small tree; scarce.
California-laurel, Oregon myrtle, Pacific myrtle, pepperwood, spice-tree, California bay tree	Wood darkens when soaked in water; high compression strength; formerly used in shipbuilding; scarce.

IMPORTED WOODS

Common Name	Notes
genuine mahogany, Honduras, Cuban, West Indian, etc., mahogany, madeira, redwood	Good durability; superb planking and trim timber.
African mahogany, mahogany	Similar to genuine mahogany.
Spanish cedar, cigar box cedar, Philippine cedar, cedro	Somewhat coarser and less dense than true mahogany; good durability and resistance to shipworms.
Philippine mahogany, lauan (dark red, light red, white), mahogany	Ranges from moderately durable to nondurable; coarse textured; moderate to poor strength properties; used for planking and trim.
genuine teak, teak	Excellent durability; superb for decking, planking and trim; becoming scarce.
angelique	Has been used for decking, planking, frames and keels; sold as a teak substitute.

Excerpted from "Wood Technology," *WoodenBoat* No. 37, November/December 1980, courtesy Richard Jagels.

Suggested Reading

The following books and articles are suggested in hopes that a few more boats will be built with a little more ease and a lot more inspiration. If you're having trouble selecting lumber or tools, or just don't know how to tackle that set of plans, we feel there's a lot to be gained from reading relevant material listed here.

Titles have been selected to direct builders to well-illustrated details and sound technical information.

Most of what's suggested is pertinent to the construction of a number of different boats. It's advice from professionals, but is geared toward the do-it-yourselfer. We encourage you to take full advantage of the experiences of others in the knowledge that it will prove beneficial. We'll wager that many of your questions already have an answer.

Books

Birmingham, Richard. *Boat Building Techniques Illustrated.* Camden, ME: International Marine Publishing Co., 1984.

Bingham, Fred P. *Practical Yacht Joinery.* Camden, ME: International Marine Publishing Co., 1983.

Blandford, Percy W. *Rigging Sail.* Blue Ridge Summit, PA: Tab Books, 1983.

British Forest Products Research Laboratory. *Woodbending Handbook.* London: Her Majesty's Stationery Office, 1970.

Bureau of Ships, U.S. Navy. *Wood: A Manual for its Use as a Shipbuilding Material.* Kingston, MA: Teaparty Books, 1983.

Chapelle, Howard I. *Boatbuilding.* New York: W.W. Norton & Co., 1969.

Collingwood, G.H. and Warren Brush. *Knowing Your Trees.* Washington: American Forestry Association, 1978.

Frid, Tage. *Tage Frid Teaches Woodworking: Joinery, Tools and Techniques.* Newtown, CT: The Taunton Press, 1979.

_____. *Tage Frid Teaches Woodworking: Shaping, Veneering, Finishing.* Newtown, CT: The Taunton Press, 1981.

The Gougeon Brothers. *The Gougeon Brothers on Boat Construction.* Bay City, MI: The Gougeon Brothers, 1980.

Guzzwell, John. *Modern Wooden Yacht Construction.* Camden, ME: International Marine Publishing Co., 1979.

Hoadley, R. Bruce. *Understanding Wood.* Newtown, CT: The Taunton Press, 1980.

Howard-Williams, Jeremy. *Sails.* Fifth Edition. Camden, ME: International Marine Publishing Co., 1983.

Hanna, Jay S. *Marine Carving Handbook.* Camden, ME: International Marine Publishing Co., 1975.

Kinney, Francis S. *Skene's Elements of Yacht Design.* New York: Dodd, Mead & Co., 1973.

Lowell, Royal. *Boatbuilding Down East.* Camden, ME: International Marine Publishing Co., 1977.

Miller, Conrad. *Your Boat's Electrical System.* New York: Hearst Books, 1981.

Nicolson, Ian. *Cold-Moulded and Strip-Planked Wood Boatbuilding.* Dobbs Ferry, NY: Sheridan House, Inc., 1983.

Payson, Harold H. *Go Build Your Own Boat!* New York: Van Nostrand Reinhold Co., 1983.

_____. *Keeping the Cutting Edge: Setting and Sharpening Hand and Power Saws.* Brooklin, ME: WoodenBoat Publications, Inc., 1983.

Rabl, S.S. *Boatbuilding in Your Own Backyard.* Cambridge, MD: Cornell Maritime Press, 1958.

Smith, Hervey Garrett. *Boat Carpentry.* New York: Van Nostrand Reinhold Co., 1965.

Steward, Robert M. *Boatbuilding Manual.* Camden, ME: International Marine Publishing Co., 1980.

Simmons, Walter J. *Building Lapstrake Canoes.* Lincolnville, ME: Duck Trap Woodworking, 1983.

_____. *Lapstrake Boatbuilding, Vol. 1.* Lincolnville, ME: Duck Trap Woodworking, 1983.

_____. *Lapstrake Boatbuilding, Vol. 2.* Camden, ME: International Marine Publishing Co., 1983.

U.S. Forest Products Laboratory. *The Encyclopedia of Wood.* New York: Sterling Publishing Co., 1980.

Vaitses, Allan H. *Lofting.* Camden, ME: International Marine Publishing Co., 1980.

Watson, Aldren A. *Hand Tools: Their Ways and Workings.* New York: W.W. Norton & Co., 1982.

Witt, Glen L. and Ken Hankinson. *Boatbuilding with Plywood.* Bellflower, CA: Glen-L Marine, 1978.

Witt, Glen L. *How to Build Boat Trailers.* Bellflower, CA: Glen-L Marine, 1967.

WoodenBoat Editors. *How to Build the Catspaw Dinghy.* Brooklin, ME: WoodenBoat Publications, Inc., 1980.

WoodenBoat Editors. *WoodenBoat: An Appreciation of the Craft.* Reading, MA: Addison-Wesley Publishing Co.,1982.

Articles in *WoodenBoat*

Adhesives

Buckley, Jennifer. "Holding Fast: Sonny Hodgdon on Glues." WB No. 59, p. 88

Jagels, Richard. "Wood Technology: Joining Wood With Adhesives." WB No. 44, p. 133

Jagels, Richard. "Wood Technology: Isocyanate Resins for Wood." WB No. 48, p. 123.

Pazereskis, John. "Icky, Sticky, Goo." WB No. 19, p. 46

Schindler, Gerald. "Adhesives and the Boatbuilder." WB No. 4, p. 47

Bedding Compounds

Boat Plans

Boatbuilding (General Information)

Boatbuilding

(How-to-build articles for boats in this catalog)

Haist, Paul. "Projection Lofting." Enlarging the lines plan to full size through projection. WB No. 51, p. 94

Lagner, Richard. "Saving Time in the Mold Loft; Pick 'Em Up with Precision." WB No. 31, p. 66

Manning, Sam. "Some Thoughts on Lofting." An introduction to lofting, its importance, and what information can be obtained from the process. WB No. 11, p. 43

————. "Lofting the Lubec Boat." A step-by-step explanation of lofting, using a specific boat as an example. WB No. 12, p. 44

McIntosh, David (Bud). "On Laying Down & Taking Off." A designer and master builder's spirited account of the procedures he follows in yacht building after years of simplifying. WB No. 11, p. 48

Minch, Dave and Ed. "Other Ways: Picking Up Through Plastic." WB No. 35, p. 95

Morris, Ralph. "Lofting by Numbers." A quick method for finding true bevels and reducing offsets from the outside of the plank to the inside. WB No. 52, p. 69

Porter, Dave. "Saving Time in the Mold Loft; Pick 'Em Up Fast." WB No. 31, p. 64

Mast and Spar Construction

Emmett, Jim. "Mast Making: Start from Scratch." A brief rundown on shaping a round solid spar. WB No. 15, p. 58

Garden, William. "The Right Jaws for Your Gaff and Boom." Details and proportions for making your own. WB No. 59, p. 100

Marsland, John. "Mast Making: The Hollow Spar." Techniques for making a round hollow spar. WB No. 15, p. 60

McIntosh, Bud. "Spars." Very comprehensive; very good. Well illustrated by Sam Manning. WB No. 60, p. 125

Pardey, Lin and Larry. "Mast Making: Building a Practical Wooden Spar." How to build simple, hollow, box-section masts. WB No. 15, p. 64

Tools

Baker, Bob. "Keep it Simple." Basic tool requirements for starting out. WB No. 32, p. 32

Curry, James. "The Nearly Forgotten Art of Making Planes." WB No. 11, p. 52

Payson, Harold. "Keeping a Cutting Edge: Handsaws." WB No. 47, p. 91

————. "Keeping a Cutting Edge: Powersaws." WB No. 48, p. 44

Note: Both the above Payson articles are included in a WoodenBoat book. (See "Suggested Bibliography of Books.")

Simmons, Walter J. "Clamps & Cleverness." Ideas on effective ways of using various clamps. WB No. 12, p. 62

WoodenBoat Editors. "Pete Culler's Workshop, Parts I and II." A look at the tools and shop layout of a master craftsman and boatbuilder. WB No. 27, p. 81; WB No. 28, p. 83

Wood: Harvesting, Milling, and Seasoning

Andersen, Doug. "Custom Sawmilling." WB No. 51, p. 106

Darr, Bob. "Milling Your Own." WB No. 37, p. 98

Day, Jane. "Harvesting Hackmatack Knees." WB No. 30, p. 66

Jagels, Richard. "Wood Technology: Sawmill Objectives— For Good Yield or Good Boats?" WB No. 38, p. 108

————. "Wood Technology: Drying Out." WB No. 23, p. 22

————. "Wood Technology: Crook Timber." WB No. 40, p. 120

Malloff, Will. "Chainsaw Lumbermaking: Natural Knees." WB No. 50, p. 38

Page, Charles. "Seasoning Science." WB No. 10, p. 39

Wood: Preservatives

Jagels, Richard. "Wood Technology: Pressure-Treated Lumber." WB No. 28, p. 94

————. "Wood Technology: Health Hazards of Wood Additives." WB No. 59, p. 111

Wood: Sources and Selection

Bielinski, Jon. "The People's Timber." WB No. 45, p. 46

Darr, Robert. "Alternatives to the Lumberyard." WB No. 35, p. 45

Jagels, Richard. "Wood Technology: Looking Behind the Grades." Three parts: WB No. 20, p. 20; WB No. 22, p. 20; WB No. 24, p. 22

————. "Wood Technology: Teak Substitutes." WB No. 27, p. 20

————. "Wood Technology: Common Names May Be Deceiving." WB No. 36, p. 89

————. "Wood Technology: Scientific Names are More Precise." WB No. 37, p. 108

————. "Wood Technology: Under-Utilized Boatbuilding Woods." Two parts. WB No. 42, p. 123; WB No. 43, p. 120.

————. "Wood Technology: Distinguishing Mahogany from the Substitutes." WB No. 55, p. 120

————. "Wood Technology: Plywood—An Engineered Wood Product." WB No. 56, p. 125

Scheffer, T.C. et al. "A Technical Comparison of Red and White Oaks." WB No. 1, p. 48

Wilson, Jon. "Making a Choice." Part I: The Domestic Woods, WB No. 9, p. 31; Part II: The Imported Woods, WB No. 10, p. 35

Ordering Information:

Plans, books, and back issues listed on these pages may be ordered from WoodenBoat, P.O. Box 78, Brooklin, ME 04616. An order form has been included in this catalog for your convenience.

Due to fluctuations in price and inventory, we suggest that you check a recent issue of WoodenBoat magazine or The WoodenBoat Store for current cost and ordering information.

Please note that *The WoodenBoat Index* (Issues 1–100) and *The WoodenBoat Index Supplement* (Issues 101–126) are highly recommended as a more comprehensive and in-depth subject guide to all that WoodenBoat has published.

WoodenBoat Plans Policies

This catalog has been designed to inform and educate readers and prospective builders. While all information has been obtained from reliable sources and we believe it to be accurate, NO WARRANTY CAN BE MADE OR SHOULD BE IMPLIED with respect to this catalog's contents. Readers are urged to rely on their own good sense and personal experience when considering any design for reasons of performance or ease of construction.

While all care has been taken with each set of plans offered, the designer and WoodenBoat DISCLAIM ALL LIABILITY for loss or injury to property or person which might occur while using these boats, including loss due to careless handling or sailing of the boat under conditions beyond its reasonable limits. We also DISCLAIM ALL LIABILITY for boats built of inferior materials, to substandard workmanship, or to specifications or construction methods other than those suggested by the designer. Plans buyers who wish to modify a design IN ANY WAY are cautioned to do so only under the guidance of a competent naval architect.

Note: Plans are sold with the understanding that one boat only may be built from each set. If you wish to build more than one boat, please write for royalty terms. Plans may not be reproduced in any form, or by electronic or mechanical means, without permission.

*General Notes on Designs

Performance section:

WoodenBoat's comments concerning the type of waters a boat is suitable for, as well as a vessel's intended capacity (number of persons), are based on the boat being used by experienced people in favorable wind and sea conditions. Owners are advised to check U.S. Coast Guard capacity regulations, where applicable.

Building Data section:

Information regarding alternative construction methods for a design means only that the hull shape would lend itself to these alternative methods. Unless otherwise noted, plans *do not* include details for modified construction, and builders must rely on their own resources.

It should also be noted that Weight/Displacement figures provided under "Particulars" are estimated for small unballasted craft without people or gear aboard.

The WoodenBoat Store

P.O. Box 78, Naskeag Road • Brooklin, Maine 04616-0078

Toll-Free U.S. & Canada:
1-800-273-SHIP (7447)

Hours: 8am–6pm EST, Mon.–Fri. (9–5 Sats. Oct.–Dec.)
24-Hour Fax: 207-359-8920 **Overseas:** Call 207-359-4647

Ordered by _____

Address _____

_____

City/State/Zip _____

Day Phone# _____

Catalog Code **V1PL**

SHIP TO — only if different than "ORDERED BY"

Name _____

Address _____

_____

City/State/Zip _____

Product #	Qty.	Item	Ship Wt.	Total

SUB TOTAL	
Maine Residents Add 6% Tax	
Regular Shipping	
Two Day Delivery	
Next Day Delivery	
International Air	
TOTAL	

Pre-payment is required. Payment MUST be in U.S. funds payable on a U.S. bank,
VISA **VISA**   MasterCard **MasterCard**   Discover **DISCOVER**   Check, or Money Orders.

CARD NUMBER

EXPIRES Month/Year (required)

SIGNATURE OF CARDHOLDER

U.S. Shipping Charges

	Zip Code up to 49999	50000+	Two Day Delivery	Next Day Delivery
Minimum	$2.00	$2.00	$7.50	$12.00
1/2 to 1 lb.	3.00	3.00	7.50	13.50
up to 2 lbs.	3.00	3.00	8.50	14.50
up to 5 lbs.	4.50	6.00	9.50	18.50
up to 10 lbs	5.00	8.00	15.50	26.00
up to 15 lbs	6.00	10.00	21.50	31.00
Add for each additional 5 lbs.	$1.00	$2.00	$5.00	$5.00

Alaska and Hawaii Priority ADD $10.00 to Two Day and Next Day Charges (No P.O. Boxes)

CANADIAN CHARGES	OVERSEAS SURFACE	OVERSEAS PRIORITY/AIR
Up to 1/2 lb. $3.00	Up to 1/2 lb. $4.00	Up to 1/2 lb. $7.00
Up to 2 lbs. 5.00	Up to 2 lbs. 7.00	Up to 1 lbs. 13.00
Up to 3 lbs. 6.50	Up to 3 lbs. 9.00	Up to 2 lbs. 22.00
Up to 4 lbs. 8.00	Up to 4 lbs. 11.00	Up to 3 lbs. 28.00
		Up to 4 lbs. 34.00
ADD $1.50 for each additional lb. PRIORITY: ADD $2.00 to Total	ADD $2.00 for each additional lb. (Allow 2-4 months for delivery)	ADD $6.00 for each additional lb.

Our Guarantee...
Satisfaction or Your Money Back!

The WoodenBoat Store

P.O. Box 78, Naskeag Road • Brooklin, Maine 04616-0078

Toll-Free U.S. & Canada:
1-800-273-SHIP (7447)

Hours: 8am–6pm EST, Mon.–Fri. (9–5 Sats. Oct.–Dec.)
24-Hour Fax: 207-359-8920 **Overseas:** Call 207-359-4647

Ordered by _____

Address _____

City/State/Zip _____

Phone# _____

Catalog Code   **V1PL**

——— SHIP TO — only if different than "ORDERED BY" ———

Name _____

Address _____

_____

City/State/Zip _____

Product #	Qty.	Item	Ship Wt.	Total

SUB TOTAL	
Maine Residents Add 6% Tax	
Regular Shipping	
Two Day Delivery	
Next Day Delivery	
International Air	
TOTAL	

Pre-payment is required. Payment MUST be in U.S. funds payable on a U.S. bank,
VISA *VISA*   MasterCard *MasterCard*   Discover *DISCOVER*   Check, or Money Orders.

CARD NUMBER

SIGNATURE OF CARDHOLDER

EXPIRES Month/Year (required)

U.S. Shipping Charges

	Zip Code up to 49999	50000+	Two Day Delivery	Next Day Delivery
Minimum	$2.00	$2.00	$7.50	$12.00
1/2 to 1 lb.	3.00	3.00	7.50	13.50
Up to 2 lbs.	3.00	3.00	8.50	14.50
Up to 5 lbs.	4.50	6.00	9.50	18.50
Up to 10 lbs	5.00	8.00	15.50	26.00
Up to 15 lbs	6.00	10.00	21.50	31.00
Add for each additional 5 lbs.	$1.00	$2.00	$5.00	$5.00

Alaska and Hawaii Priority ADD $10.00 to Two Day and Next Day Charges (No P.O. Boxes)

CANADIAN CHARGES	OVERSEAS SURFACE	OVERSEAS PRIORITY/AIR
Up to 1/2 lb. $3.00	Up to 1/2 lb. $4.00	Up to 1/2 lb. $7.00
Up to 2 lbs. 5.00	Up to 2 lbs. 7.00	Up to 1 lbs. 13.00
Up to 3 lbs. 6.50	Up to 3 lbs. 9.00	Up to 2 lbs. 22.00
Up to 4 lbs. 8.00	Up to 4 lbs. 11.00	Up to 3 lbs. 28.00
		Up to 4 lbs. 34.00
ADD $1.50 for each additional lb. **PRIORITY:** ADD $2.00 to Total	ADD $2.00 for each additional lb. (Allow 2-4 months for delivery)	ADD $6.00 for each additional lb.

Our Guarantee...
Satisfaction or Your Money Back!

The WoodenBoat Store

P.O. Box 78, Naskeag Road • Brooklin, Maine 04616-0078

Toll-Free U.S. & Canada:
1-800-273-SHIP (7447)

Hours: 8am–6pm EST, Mon.–Fri. (9–5 Sats. Oct.–Dec.)
24-Hour Fax: 207-359-8920 **Overseas:** Call 207-359-4647

Ordered by _____

Address _____

City/State/Zip _____

Phone# _____

Catalog Code	V1PL

SHIP TO — only if different than "ORDERED BY"

Name _____

Address _____

_____

City/State/Zip _____

Product #	Qty.	Item	Ship Wt.	Total

SUB TOTAL	
Maine Residents Add 6% Tax	
Regular Shipping	
Two Day Delivery	
Next Day Delivery	
International Air	
TOTAL	

Pre-payment is required. Payment MUST be in U.S. funds payable on a U.S. bank,
VISA **VISA**   MasterCard **MasterCard**   Discover **DISCOVER**   Check, or Money Orders.

CARD NUMBER

SIGNATURE OF CARDHOLDER

EXPIRES Month/Year (required)

U.S. Shipping Charges

	Zip Code up to 49999	50000+	Two Day Delivery	Next Day Delivery
Minimum	$2.00	$2.00	$7.50	$12.00
½ to 1 lb.	3.00	3.00	7.50	13.50
1 to 2 lbs.	3.00	3.00	8.50	14.50
2 to 5 lbs.	4.50	6.00	9.50	18.50
5 to 10 lbs	5.00	8.00	15.50	26.00
10 to 15 lbs	6.00	10.00	21.50	31.00

Add for each additional 5 lbs. $1.00 $2.00 $5.00 $5.00

Alaska and Hawaii Priority ADD $10.00 to Two Day and Next Day Charges (No P.O. Boxes)

CANADIAN CHARGES

Up to ½ lb.	$3.00
Up to 2 lbs.	5.00
Up to 3 lbs.	6.50
Up to 4 lbs.	8.00

ADD $1.50 for each additional lb.
PRIORITY:
ADD $2.00 to Total

OVERSEAS SURFACE

Up to ½ lb.	$4.00
Up to 2 lbs.	7.00
Up to 3 lbs.	9.00
Up to 4 lbs.	11.00

ADD $2.00 for each additional lb.
(Allow 2-4 months for delivery)

OVERSEAS PRIORITY/AIR

Up to ½ lb.	$7.00
Up to 1 lbs.	13.00
Up to 2 lbs.	22.00
Up to 3 lbs.	28.00
Up to 4 lbs.	34.00

ADD $6.00 for each additional lb.

Our Guarantee... Satisfaction or Your Money Back!